Take your first step. Record a video of you taking the pledge, then post it on social with the hashtag #CredibilityNationPledge.

Credibility Nation Pledge:

I pledge to live credibly every day without hate in my life. I strive to be a good human and make this a better planet for myself, my family, and for other people's families in this generation and the next.

Testimonials

On Mitchell as a Human:
"It's not often that you can meet someone that gives you the space to really tap into your own power and Mitchell Levy does that. He's an extraordinary human being."
~ **Lisa Mininni**

"I actually felt like I mattered . . . like I was a real person, a real human, and not just someone else that was going to go on and be interviewed before another person and another person to follow. And that made it a very special moment for me."
~ **Nicola Hunt**

"Mitchell understands how to help people to be better and gives you that valuable feedback. I don't believe that Mitchell leads anyone down the road of any sort of projects that doesn't have your best interest in mind." ~ **Dr. Jeffrey Magee**

"I gotta tell you, Mitchell is one of the coolest guys you'll ever sit down with . . . He's fun to work with, easy to talk with . . . I've had a lot of fun here in these past few minutes and I'm excited about continuing to work with him." ~ **Timothy Jones**

"Mitchell Levy is one of my favorite people. He's extremely smart, compassionate, generous with his time, a master marketer and promoter. And I always love talking and working with Mitchell." ~ **Wendy Marx**

On Credibility:
"In today's world, we all need to work on our credibility and Mitchell Levy, I was with him for what? Four minutes? And he helps me see the way I do my work in a totally different way that I'm gonna take with me." ~ **Cali Yost**

"Mitchell Levy is an excellent consultant when it comes to helping you think about your thought leadership, your credibility, your brand, all of the above."
~ **Melissa Lamson**

"I would say Mitchell Levy is the man with the dope hat and the best Credust in the world. As the Global Credibility Expert, he's helping all his clients to get in front of the right people and be seen and heard by the right people. And most of all, create that clarity and intensity of connection." ~ **Ellen Moore**

"What I love about Mitchell Levy is he is an absolute seventh dan black belt on understanding and implementing one of the most corporate principles of influence, and that is to become influential and credible in your own right." ~ **Teresa de Grosbois**

"I just spent a few minutes with Mitchell Levy. We were shooting a credreel, and this man is a genius when it comes to spreading your Credust and obtaining credibility. This video presentation, he just put together four key questions that help you and help others understand who you are and help you get a laser of focus on where your credibility lies." ~ **V. Lee Henson**

On Clarity:
"Mitchell Levy is Mr. Clarity, and I can tell you he's one of the best that I've seen because he gets it quickly. And he speaks with perfect clarity. He walks his talk."
~ **Gary Hernbroth**

"Just had a fantastic interview with Mitchell Levy about my CPoP, my customer point of pain. Mitchell's got a really, really nice sense of what messaging is gonna work well. Like, 'let's clear out all the crap' and get you really focused on these six words that are gonna get people's attention and connect with your target audience." ~ **Susan Thompson**

"I really want to thank Mitchell Levy because I recognize the importance of being able to present myself to others in a way that's succinct and really gets me across . . . And Mitchell has really been helpful in guiding me to be succinct, to the point, and to be able to get my message." ~ **Norman Wolfe**

"Mitchell Levy gave me more clarity. He shared the kind truth, which I'm always grateful for. You told me what I needed to hear vs. what I wanted to hear so that we could put together a good product out." ~ **Bobby Herrera**

"Mitchell's level of clarity helped me make my message even more clear. Clarity is power, and if you want to clarify your message and you want to have some Credust, he's the master." ~ **Roger Salam**

Scan the QR code or use this link to watch the video testimonials:
https://aha.pub/CredibilityTestimonials

Did you take the pledge yet? https://CredibilityNation.com/Pledge

Credibility Nation

For Professionals Who Want to Be Seen as Credible

Mitchell Levy

THiNK*aha*®

An Actionable Credibility Journal

E-mail: info@thinkaha.com
20660 Stevens Creek Blvd., Suite 210
Cupertino, CA 95014

Please go to
https://aha.pub/CredibilityNationAHAs
to read this AHAbook and to share the
individual AHA messages that resonate with you.

Published by THiNKaha®
20660 Stevens Creek Blvd., Suite 210,
Cupertino, CA 95014
https://thinkaha.com
E-mail: info@thinkaha.com

First & Second Printing: October 2020
Hardcover ISBN: 978-1-61699-378-8 1-61699-378-2
Paperback ISBN: 978-1-61699-377-1 1-61699-377-4
eBook ISBN: 978-1-61699-376-4 1-61699-376-6
Place of Publication: Silicon Valley, California, USA
Paperback Library of Congress Number: 2020917222

Trademarks

All terms mentioned in this book that are known to be trademarks or service marks have been appropriately capitalized. Neither THiNKaha, nor any of its imprints, can attest to the accuracy of this information. Use of a term in this book should not be regarded as affecting the validity of any trademark or service mark.

https://mitchelllevy.com/credibilitynation/ahapubs shows all the locations that the short aha.pub URLs direct to.

Warning and Disclaimer

Every effort has been made to make this book as complete and as accurate as possible. The information provided is on an "as is" basis. The author(s), publisher, and their agents assume no responsibility for errors or omissions. Nor do they assume liability or responsibility to any person or entity with respect to any loss or damages arising from the use of information contained herein.

Book Summary & Introduction

For many years, a silent and important war has been fought between two nations.

On the one side, there's Credibility Nation, which is composed of humans who go about life and their business with credibility and servant leadership. On the other side, there's Dubious Nation, which is composed of humans who live and conduct their business with self-interest as their highest priority.

Dubious Nation is on a winning streak and is vanquishing Credibility Nation a thousand times over. It's shocking to see how many people are forgetting how important it is to live and transact business in a credible way.

I believe that there's still hope. There's still a way for Credibility Nation to win. It definitely won't be easy and it won't happen in a day, but we can do it.

The path toward credibility starts with seeing and acknowledging that the world has changed.

We used to live in a village economy where people did business with a handshake. That was a time when people exchanged goods and services for other goods and services without using money. In that kind of economy, when a proprietor's product didn't live up to expectations, the villagers would either self-correct or ostracize.

After the village economy, we transitioned to and are now in the industrial age. Didn't we leave the industrial age and move into the Internet age? Sort of, but not really. What we've done is to primarily use technology to extend the processes, rules, and approaches to business and life that were developed in the industrial age.

The industrial age is a time where power and status are everything. The higher you rise on the corporate ladder, no matter what means you took to get there, the more successful and happier you become. The industrial age is dominated by self-satisfaction and self-interest.

Today, we're slowly transitioning to the global village. It is similar to the village economy, with the big difference being our reach. We can now reach and need to be aware of millions of people from around the world.

The keys to success and happiness in the global village are credibility and relationships. Since technology has enabled us to connect with more people, how we live and do business can easily be seen. Thus, presenting ourselves as credibly as we can allows others to want to get to know, like, and trust us.

I wrote this book with the intention of enlightening humanity about what credibility truly is, how important it is as we move forward to the future, and how we can transform ourselves into credible humans.

My hope is that this book will serve as a wake-up call, a reminder, and a blueprint for those who want to join me in this movement toward credibility.

Now, take a look at yourself. Are you more in alignment with Credibility Nation than Dubious Nation? Or maybe it's the other way around.

If you feel like you're more dubious than credible, you're not alone. Don't worry. There's always room for change and transformation. There will always be people who will lend you a helping hand and guide you toward credibility.

The doors of Credibility Nation will always be open to those who are willing and ready to transform themselves into better human beings. It's up to you to take that first step. Will you take it? We need you to be the human you know in your heart you want to be. Please join me in this epic battle against Dubious Nation.

The goal in my lifetime is to tip the scale.

Dedication

I dedicate this book—

To those who wish to be proactive in creating and leaving behind a better way of living—where credible interactions are the norm—for today and for future generations.

To the members of my team and their families who helped make this happen.

To my family because they are the foundation from which I see the world.

Did you take the pledge yet? https://CredibilityNation.com/Pledge

Acknowledgements

I have an amazing team and couldn't have done the research and the book without them. I've spent many evenings with Nikka Ann Alejandro on writing and Jenilee Maniti on project management. I also want to thank Nikka, Kharen Basa, and Alfred Ramos for driving the interview process and Cristina Rafol for driving online courses and the membership community.

I want to acknowledge C. Lee Smith (**https://aha.pub/CLeeSmithCred**), who graciously signed up as the first governor of Credibility Nation and who asked that I publish a book on the credibility of salespeople (*SalesCred*, THiNKaha). It was amazingly fun and valuable brainstorming ideas for both books. I'm excited about the contribution that *SalesCred* and *Credibility Nation* will have on the world.

I also need to acknowledge my amazing clients, friends, and family whom I have spent time with while shaping my thoughts. They have all supported me in the evolution of who I am today.

Finally, I would like to thank everyone who has been a part of the credibility interviews. Those mentioned below also agreed to be listed in this book:

Aaron Weller, Achim Nowak, Adam Gordon, Adam Kipnes, Adam Lewis Walker, Adam Torres, Adrean Turner, Adrienne Barker, Ajax Greene, Alain Hunkins, Alan Gellman, Alan Jackson, Alex Melen, Alex Sharpe, Alexanne Stone, Alicia Castillo Holley, Allan Fine, Alyssa Dver, Ande Lyons, Andoni Silva, Andrea Adams-Miller, Andrea Feinberg, Andrea Simon, Andrew Aken, Andrew Izumi, Andy Goldstrom, Angela Proffitt, Angelique Rewersw, Anna Mandell, Anne Beninghof, Anthony Hogan, Anuschka Ollnow, Asha Mankowska, Athol Foden, Avis Jones-DeWeever, Axel Meierhoefer.

Barbara Weaver Smith, Barry Moltz, Belinda Ellsworth, Ben Baker, Ben Gay III, Bernadette Boas, Bernie Borges, Beth Barany, Beth Bridges, Beth Masterman, Betty Lochner, Bill Amirault, Bill Benoist, Bill Coletti, Bill Reed, Bill Wallace, Bob Britton, Bob Geller, Bob Musial, Bonnie Clipper, Brad Friedman, Brandon Dawson, Brenda Christensen, Brenda Cross, Brian Nelson, Brian Olds, Brian Rollo, Brian Schulman, Brian Swift, Brigette Iarrusso, Brooke Erol, Bryan Mattimore, Byrd Baggett, C. Lee Smith, C. Mike Lewis, Cali Yost, Cami Baker, Carl Friesen, Carl Pritchard, Carl Utter, Carole O'Brien, Carolina Billings, Carolyn Landesman, Chad Cooper, Charlene DeCesare, Cheryl Moses, Chris Bryant, Chuck Garcia, Chuck Hall, Clay Staires, Connie Pheiff, Cornelia Gamlem, Coylette James, Craig Dunkerley.

Dan Goodwin, Dan Riley, Daniel Ramsay, Danny Hadas, Darelyn Mitsch, Dave Kenney, Dave Roby, Daven Michaels, David Bryson, David Finkel, David Fradin, David Goldsmith, David Grebow, David Kauffman, David Lukas, David Meerman Scott, David Polinchock, Deb Beroset, Debbie Hoffman, Debbra Sweet, Deborah Dubree, Deborah Krier, Deidra Cox, Devin Johnson, Diane Conklin, Dianna Booher, Dilip Saraf, Dolores Hirschmann, Don Williams, Dorinda Vance, Dorothy Martin-Neville, Doug Harris, Douglas Spencer, Dov Baron, Dr. Doug Firebaugh, Dr. Jane Goldner, Dr. Jeffrey Magee, Dr. John Oda, Dr. Karen Jacobson, Dr. Michelle Reina, Dr. Nekeshia Hammond, Dr. Rachel Headley, Dr. Raman K. Attri, Dr. Susan Duffy, Duane Morrow, Dwaine Canova.

Ed Brenegar, Ed Brzychcy, Elisse Barnes, Ellen Grace Henson, Ely Delaney, Emmanuel Eliason, Eric Kaufmann, Eugene Buff, Evan Dash, Evan Hackel, Felicia Slattery, Flo Falayi, Fred McMurray, Freda Drake, Gary Hernbroth, Genevieve Piturro, George Donald Miller, Gerard Dache, Gilmore Crosby, Gordon Tredgold, Greg Williams, Gretchen Gagel, Helena Demuynck, Hema Vyas, Holly Duckworth, Holly Green, Howard Fox, Iman Aghay, Ira Ozer.

Jack Malcolm, Jack Monson, Jack Phillips, Jackie Lapin, Jacob Engel, JacQueline, Jake Carlson, Jake Jorgovan, James Hotaling, James Woeber, Jamie Mustard, Jamie Palmer, Jared Brick, Jason Collett, Jason Kanigan, Jason Safford, Jay McKeever, Jeff Barnes, Jeff Butler, Jeff Munn, Jeff Shavitz, Jeffrey Pelletier, Jennifer Fondrevay, Jennifer Hough, Jennifer McGinley, Jennifer Radke, Jennifer Vessels, Jerry Phillips, Jessica Dewell, Jessica Matthews, Jessica Yarbrough, Jim Britt, Jim Janosik, Jim Schleckser, Jim Waszak, Jo Dodds, Jo Moffatt, Jo Skipper, Jodi Daniels, Joe Folkman, John Ballis, John Bartold, John Bates, John Bernard, John Bianchi, John Coles, John Courtney, John Farley, John Sigmon, John Spence, John Vuong, Jon Ferrara, Jon Wuebben, Jonathan Stone, Jory Fisher, Joseph Flahiff, Joseph Ruiz, Joseph Siecinski, Josephine Bellaccomo, Josh Elledge, Josh Fonger, Josh Steimle, Judith Briles, Juliet Easton, Justin Hibbard, Justin Lokitz, JV Crum III.

Kaelen Revense, Kami Huyse, Kare Anderson, Karen Brown, Karen McGregor, Karin Hurt, Karthik Nagendra, Kathy Letendre, Kelly Helmuth, Kelly Primus, Kelvin McCree, Ken Homer, Ken Judy, Ken Kilday, Keri Jaehnig, Kevin Eikenberry, Kevin Wayne Johnson, Kieran Flanagan, Kiesha King-Brown, Kim Smith, Kim Svoboda, Kim Walsh Phillips, Kimberly Bonner, Kimberly Carlson, Kimberly Wiefling, Kris Yagel, Laleh Hancock, Lashondra Graves, Laura Jack, Laura Patterson, Laura Rubinstein, Lauren Cohen, Laurie Seymour, Leah Olszewski, Lee Henson, Leila Blauner, Leonard Marchese, Leslie Kushner, Lisa Fey, Lisa Manyoky, Lisa McDonald, Lisa Mininni, Lori Karpman, Lou Diamond, Lucie Newcomb, Luke Acree, Luni Libes, Lydia Sugarman, Lynn Hidy, Lynn Scheurell, Lynnea Hagen.

Mali Phonpadith, Manny Wolfe, Marcia Daszko, Marcia Reynolds, Marcus Aurelius Anderson, Mari-Lou Nidle, Marianne Roux, Marie Zimenoff, Marika Flatt, Mario Martinez, Mark Amtower, Mark Aylward, Mark Babbitt, Mark Bowser, Mark Green, Mark Maes, Mark Samuel, Mark Villareal, Marki Lemons Ryhal, Mary Dee, Mary Foltz, Mary Henderson, Mary Lippitt, Maryellen Stockton, Matthew McGregor, Mauri Schwartz, Mei Lin Fung, Melissa Lamson, Michael Griego, Michael Holloway, Michael Lee, Michael Roub, Michael Yinger, Michele Malo, Mike Bosworth, Mike Gospe, Mike O'Neil, Mike Skrypnek, Mike Stickler, Mikki Williams, Mitch Russo, Mitchell Bolnick, Mitzi Perdue, Molly Mandelberg.

Nadene Joy, Natalie Grogan, Nathan Kievman, Naveen Lakkur, Neil Anderson, Neil Gordon, Neil McDonnell, Neil Thompson, Nettie Owens, Neysha Arcelay, Nicky Billou, Nicola Hunt, Nicole Jansen, Noah Koff, Norman Wolfe, Pam Hurley, Pam Thomas, Pascale Brady, Patrice Tanaka, Patricia Jesperson, Patrick Reilly, Patti Phillips, Paul D'Souza, Paul Rosenberg, Paula Peralta, Per Sjofors, Philippe Bouissou, Praveen Puri, Professor M.S. Rao, Quinn Ferrall, R. Shawn McBride, Raj Prasad, Ramon Ray, Randall Dobbins, Randall Englund, Randy Kirk, Ray Makela, Rebecca Hulse, Regina Bergman, Rene Johnson, Richard Krawczyk, Richard McPartlin, Richard Shuster, Rita Burgett-Martell, RJ Nicolosi, Rob Wyse, Robert Pizzini, Robert Rose, Roberta Matuson, Roger Dooley, Roger Knecht, Roger Salam, Rohit Talwar, Ron Mitchell, Rosemary Coates, Ryan Dohrn, Ryan Foland.

Sal Silvester, Sandra Costéja Bos, Sarah Lawrence, Scott Crabtree, Scott Ingram, Scott Messer, Scott Schilling, Sean Erwin, Sharon McCollick, Sharon McIntosh, Shawn Hessinger, Shayna Pellino, Shel Horowitz, Shenan Reed, Shontina Gladney, Sonya Sigler, Stan Phelps, Stephan Thieringer, Stephanie Angelo, Steve Rosenbaum, Steve Sapato, Steven Bowen, Steven Crawford, Sue Tidswell, Susan Fennema, Susan Fowler, Susan Thompson, Sylvain Rochon, Sylvia Puentes.

Tad Stephens, Tameika Isaac Devine, Tammi Pickle, Tanja Barth, Tatsuya Nakagawa, Ted Riter, Ted Santos, Terence Jackson, Teresa de Grosbois, Teresa Nichols, Teri Johnson, Terri Levine, Terrlyn Curry Avery, Terry Brock, Terry Monaghan, Terryn Barill, Theresa Gale, Thom Harrison, Thom Shea, Tim Gaynor, Tim Hagen, Tim Ringgold, Tim Steele, Timothy Jones, Timothy Morgan, Timothy Sullivan, Todd Cherches, Todd Wilms, Tom Beal, Tom Matzen, Tommy Breedlove, Tracey Lawrence, Tracey Richardson, Traci Porterfield, Tracy Repchuk, Tracy Roesch Williams, Tricia Benn, Vera Anderson, Vera Jones, Vicki Suiter, Virgilia Virjoghe, Viveka von Rosen, Wade Pearse, Wael Zaki, Wendy Marx, Wes Schaeffer, Whitney Gordon-Mead, Whitney Johnson, Whitney Vosburgh, Will Bachman.

A THiNKaha book is not your typical book. It's a whole lot more while being a whole lot less. Scan the QR code, or use this link to watch me talk about this new evolutionary style of book: https://aha.pub/THiNKahaSeries

How to Read a THiNKaha® Book

A Note from the Publisher

The AHAthat/THiNKaha series was crafted to deliver content the way humans process information in today's world. Short, sweet, and to the point while delivering powerful, lasting impact.

The content is designed and presented in ways to appeal to visual, auditory, and kinesthetic personality types. Each section contains AHA messages, lines for notes, and a meme that summarizes that section. You should also scan the QR code, or click on the link, to watch a video of the author talking about that section.

This book is contextual in nature. Although the words won't change, their meaning will every time you read it as your context will. Be ready, you will experience your own AHA moments as you read. The AHA messages are designed to be stand-alone actionable messages that will help you think differently. Items to consider as you're reading include:

1. It should only take less than an hour to read the first time. When you're reading, write one to three action items that resonate with you in the underlined areas.
2. Mark your calendar to re-read it again.
3. Repeat step #1 and mark one to three additional AHA messages that resonate. As they will most likely be different, this is a great time to reflect on the messages that resonated with you during your last reading.
4. Sprinkle credust on the author and yourself by sharing the AHA messages from this book socially from the AHAthat platform https://aha.pub/CredibilityNationAHAs.

After reading this THiNKaha book, marking your AHA messages, rereading it, and marking more AHA messages, you'll begin to see how this book contextually applies to you. We advocate for continuous, lifelong learning and this book will help you transform your AHAs into action items with tangible results.

Mitchell Levy, Global Credibility Expert
publisher@thinkaha.com

THiNKaha®

Did you take the pledge yet? https://CredibilityNation.com/Pledge

Contents

CTA (Credibility Nation Pledge) 1

Testimonials 2

Book Summary & Introduction 7

Dedication 9

Acknowledgments 11

Preface (Who This Book Is For) 20

Prologue 21

Credibility Definition 23

Section I
What Is Credibility and Why Is It Important? 25

BEING KNOWN as a Pillar of Credibility. 35

Section II
Clearly Articulate Your Audience and Their Pain Point 37

Section III
Continually Reinforce Your Presence with
Who You Are and Your Credibility 55

BEING LIKEABLE as a Pillar of Credibility. 71

Section IV
The Magic of Credust 75

Section V
Show Up When You Show Up 87

BEING TRUSTWORTHY as a Pillar of Credibility.   **103**

Section VI
Reinforcing Your Commitment to Being a Genuine Human   107

Section VII
Continual Growth with Curiosity, Coachability,
and Lifelong Learning   123

Section VIII
A Life Worth Living   133

Appendices   **143**

Appendix A
Bonus AHA Messages from Guests   145

Appendix B
Credust Index   147

Appendix C
About the Nonprofit That Credibility Nation Is Supporting   151

Appendix D
The Hierarchy of Sales Credibility by C. Lee Smith   153

Appendix E
Ten Best CPoPs from Those Interviewed   157

Appendix F
Ten Ways to Enhance Your Credibility   159

Appendix G
Ten Things You Do to Hurt Your Credibility   163

Appendix H
Ten Best AHA Messages from
"BEing Seen and BEing Heard as a Thought Leader"   165

Appendix I
The Interview Process and Methodology   169

Appendix J
Showing Up with Respect for a Live Show   175

Epilogue   **177**

About the Author   **179**

Preface

Who This Book Is For

This book is for those who want to leave a better world for future generations.

With the help of Bill Wallace (*Being a Catalyst for Success*, THiNKaha, https://aha.pub/BillWallaceCred), I changed my belief system. I used to think that there were only two types of people in the world: those who viewed the world as glass half full and those who viewed it as glass half empty.

Bill helped me to see a third type of person because he describes himself as someone whose glass is overflowing. Thank you, Bill. You are an amazing human!

A natural extension of Bill's thinking is someone whose glass is overturned and glued to the table—the opposite of Bill.

A simple view of humans classifies them into four categories:

1) **Glass half full**
   Those who see the good in every situation.

2) **Glass half empty**
   Those who see the bad in every situation.

3) **Glass overflowing**
   A servant leader who wants to continually support and serve others.

4) **Glass overturned and glued to the table**
   Those who have chips on their shoulders and derive pleasure in making other people unhappy.

Prologue

Q: What got Mitchell Levy to conduct 500 credibility interviews?

I have lived a really beautiful life so far. I've been in Silicon Valley for thirty-five years. I've been happily married for thirty-one years. I have a beautiful son. Work-wise, I've done lots of really cool things.

Here are some highlights from my bio:

- Sat on a board of a public company for nine years.
- Ran four CEO networking groups for a decade.
- Created four different executive business programs at Silicon Valley universities.
- Created over twenty companies.
- Ran four conferences for COMDEX.
- As a book publisher, I've published over 850 books since 2005.

Having been in Silicon Valley as long as I have, having focused on thought leadership for twenty-five years, I felt comfortable calling myself a Global Credibility Expert. That said, I wanted to do something that really reinforced that brand.

I woke up one day and thought, "Napoleon Hill, 500 Millionaires, Think and Grow Rich"—"Mitchell Levy, 500 thought leaders, interviewing them on credibility." At the time, I had no idea what the title of my book would be. I then went to my team and started talking about doing the research.

One of my superpowers is to build systems. As a CEO, I could have built the model, thrown it to the team, and said, "Do this." What I did instead was to actively get my team involved.

The hope of many entrepreneurs is that their team does a great job while also being rainmakers. They want their team to be excited about the mission, the overall goals of the company and what they're doing and take personal responsibility for doing the right thing to help drive success of the company.

So, instead of driving the build myself, I let the team build it. This took five months instead of one to two, but it was absolutely worth it.

We ran a couple of months of practice where we conducted four to five interviews each and then went full-steam ahead.

It's been a fun ride, and doing the 500 interviews has been absolutely amazing.

What I was originally hoping to achieve by doing the interviews was that someone would look at me and go, "Hey, yes! That's it! You are the Global Credibility Expert!"

What actually occurred around interview forty was that I entered flow. I knew the value of what I was contributing. I knew what this would ultimately be. I realized that I didn't need anyone to tell me who I am. I just know who I am.

This is a topic that's so valuable, so important, so vital, I just feel it. The feedback I get from those interviewed and the love that they share is just so amazing.

So, when you look at the book and see the stats, these are all statistically significant and reinforce the qualitative feedback from the research.

What I tried to bring out in the book was the reactions I received from the interviewees and the significant effect they have had on my life.

This is how the birth of Credibility Nation came about. It was born out of the desire to do something that would add credibility to my title, but it turned into an interesting way of living.

Scan the QR code or use this link to watch the prologue video: https://aha.pub/CredibilityNationPrologue

Credibility Definition:

THE THREE PILLARS OF CREDIBILITY

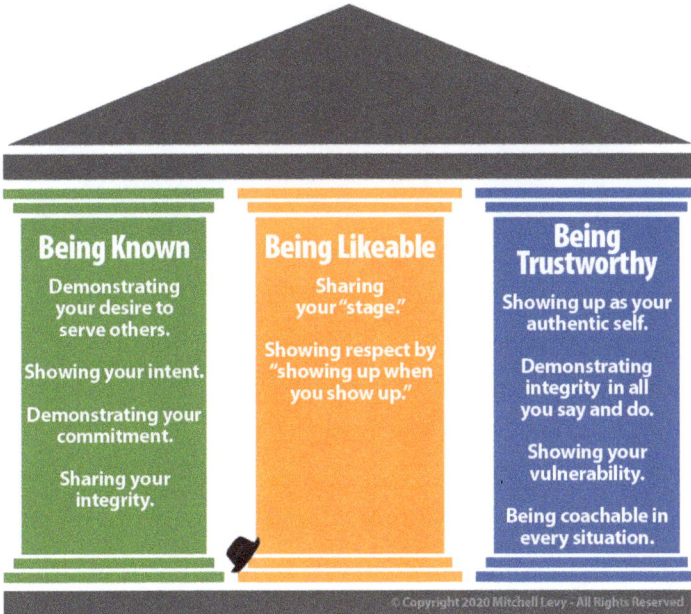

Being Known

Demonstrating your desire to serve others.

Showing your intent.

Demonstrating your commitment.

Sharing your integrity.

Being Likeable

Sharing your "stage."

Showing respect by "showing up when you show up."

Being Trustworthy

Showing up as your authentic self.

Demonstrating integrity in all you say and do.

Showing your vulnerability.

Being coachable in every situation.

Credibility is being known, being likeable, and being trusted.

. . . Whereas **being known** is demonstrating your desire to serve others, as well as transparently showing your intent, demonstrating your commitment, and sharing your integrity.

. . . Whereas **being likeable** is transparently sharing your "stage" and showing respect by "showing up when you show up."

. . . Whereas **being trustworthy** is showing up as your authentic self, demonstrating integrity in all you say and do, showing your vulnerability, and being coachable in every situation.

The quality of how you are known, liked, and trusted is your credibility.

THE THREE PILLARS OF CREDIBILITY

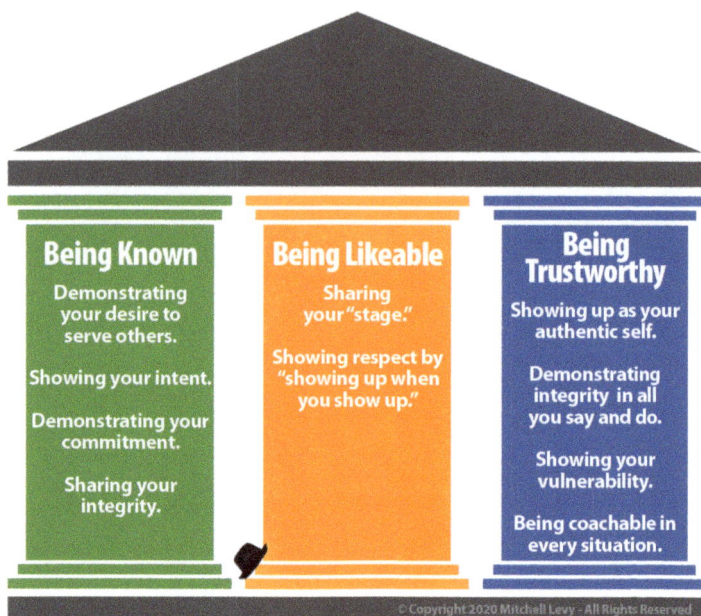

Being Known

Demonstrating your desire to serve others.

Showing your intent.

Demonstrating your commitment.

Sharing your integrity.

Being Likeable

Sharing your "stage."

Showing respect by "showing up when you show up."

Being Trustworthy

Showing up as your authentic self.

Demonstrating integrity in all you say and do.

Showing your vulnerability.

Being coachable in every situation.

Share the AHA messages from this book socially by going to
https://aha.pub/CredibilityNationAHAs.

Scan the QR code or use this link to watch the section videos and more on this section topic:
https://aha.pub/CredibilityNationSVs

Section I

What Is Credibility and Why Is It Important?

Credibility is one of the key factors to succeed in business and in life. It is what your prospects and customers (those you serve) look for when deciding whom they should do business with. Without it, you do not have a business.

So, what is credibility?

The word "credibility" is only one-third accurate in the dictionary today. The dictionary says that credibility is "the quality of being trusted." Credibility and trust are not the same thing. After having interviewed 500 thought leaders about credibility, I have learned that credibility is bigger and more powerful than that.

> Here is my simple definition of credibility. It is being known, being likeable, and being trusted (see **https://mitchelllevy.com/credibility/**).

The three pillars of credibility are discussed in this book and are broken into two sections each. The intrinsic and expressed demonstration of those three pillars are the defining components of your success going forward.

In today's world, people do business with those they know, like, and trust—in other words, those who are credible. I believe that it's extremely important for you to demonstrate credibility in everything you do. There are two reasons for this:

1. Your competition is bigger now than it's ever been.
2. It's harder and harder to hide from past indiscretions!

Technology has allowed people from around the world to communicate with each other. Everyone has access to a microphone and a camera. This means that anyone in the world can be your competition. If you're not actively demonstrating and showcasing your credibility and your competition is, whom do you think your prospects will want to do business with?

Not you!

Credibility is living in a world that's a whole lot more fun than what many people deal with today. It's a world in which you are living your purpose. It's a world where people **know**, **like**, and **trust** you for who you are and what you do because you're adding value to them and to those around them.

At the end of the day, credibility comes down to the promises you make and the believability you have for delivering on those promises. Are you clear about what you said and how you said it so that there's no ambiguity?

A big part of credibility is clarity. How do you answer the question when someone asks, "What do you do?" Does it take you five or ten minutes to answer? In a world where we're inundated with content, somebody who takes ten or twenty minutes to answer this simple question may not be considered someone who is likeable or trustworthy.

Credibility is having clarity of purpose, reason, and communication. Part of **being known**, **being likeable**, and **being trustworthy** is living a life where those who see you know immediately who you are and what you do.

The quality of how you are **known**, **liked**, and **trusted** is your credibility. Your credibility and how you go about sharing it is what sets you apart from your competition. Credibility is what will help you succeed in both business and in life.

1

#Credibility is crucial in business. Without it, you do not have a business. It is what your prospects and customers (those you serve) look for when deciding whom they should do business with. #CredibilityNation https://aha.pub/MitchellLevy

_____

_____

_____

2

According to the dictionary, credibility is the demonstration of trust. That's only 1/3 of what it really is! #Credibility is being known, being likeable, and being trustworthy (see https://MitchellLevy.com/credibility/). -Mitchell Levy

_____

_____

_____

3

#Credibility is demonstrated by living your purpose.
#CredibilityNation https://aha.pub/MitchellLevy

_____

_____

_____

4

#Credibility is demonstrated by the promises that you make and the believability you have in delivering your promises. #CredibilityNation
https://aha.pub/MitchellLevy

_____

_____

_____

5

#Credibility is not just what you say. It's not just what you do. It's how you act when you have a choice. Do you follow the shiny object, or do you stick with your core values? #CredibilityNation
https://aha.pub/MitchellLevy

_____

_____

_____

6

#Credibility is when a friend recommends you to one of their friends because they have a 100-percent certainty that you will not let them down. #CredibilityNation https://aha.pub/MitchellLevy

_____

_____

_____

7

Your competition is significantly greater than it's ever been. With a camera and a microphone, anyone in the world can be your competition. How are you responding? #CredibilityNation
https://aha.pub/MitchellLevy

_____

_____

_____

8

If you don't want to talk about yourself and your #Credibility and your competition does, who's going to get the job? Not you! #CredibilityNation
https://aha.pub/MitchellLevy

_____

_____

_____

9

If you're not presenting yourself asynchronously as #Credible, your potential customers won't get to you know you better and may not ever give you the chance to spend the time with them synchronously. #CredibilityNation https://aha.pub/MitchellLevy

_____

_____

_____

10

If the price point is large enough, your goal for obtaining your next customer is to get into a one-on-one conversation. How do you make sure you get into that conversation? #Credibility https://aha.pub/MitchellLevy

_____

_____

_____

11

When #Credibility is in place, the ability to forge ahead with business partnerships is significantly faster (e.g., the speed of a handshake). https://aha.pub/MitchellLevy #CredibilityNation

_____

_____

_____

12

Credibility is having clarity of purpose, reason, and communication. It's when people know, like, and trust you for who you are and the value you bring to the table. #CredibilityNation https://aha.pub/MitchellLevy

_____

_____

_____

THE THREE PILLARS OF CREDIBILITY

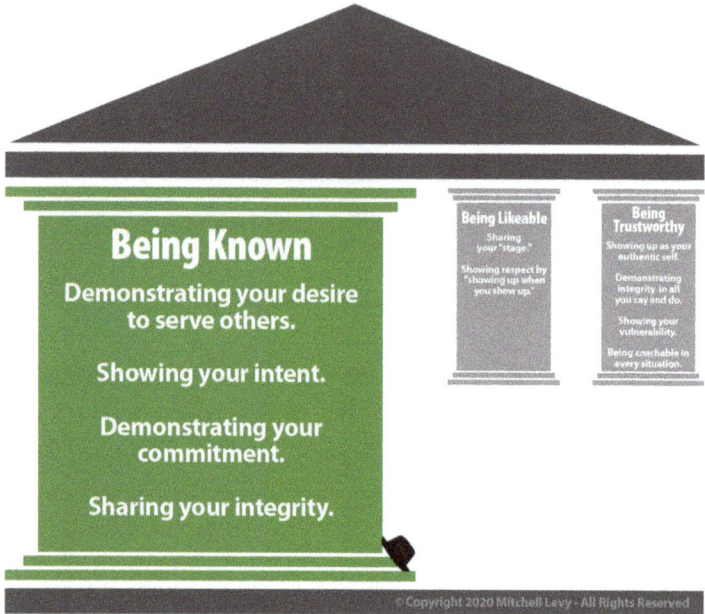

Being Known

Demonstrating your desire
to serve others.

Showing your intent.

Demonstrating your
commitment.

Sharing your integrity.

Being Likeable
Sharing
your "stage."

Showing respect by
"showing up when
you show up."

Being Trustworthy
Showing up as your
authentic self.

Demonstrating
integrity in all
you say and do.

Showing your
vulnerability.

Being coachable in
every situation.

Share the AHA messages from this book socially by going to
https://aha.pub/CredibilityNationAHAs.

*Scan the QR code or use this link to watch the video
on BEING KNOWN as a Pillar of Credibility:*
https://aha.pub/BeingKnown

BEING KNOWN as a Pillar of Credibility.
Does your *community* see who you *really* are and how you serve?

With the phrase, **"being known, being likeable, and being trustworthy,"** most humans assume what is meant by **being known**. They assume it's that others **know of** you and that they **know** your name. That is not what is meant in this book.

> "**Knowing of** you is not **knowing** you!"

It's important to note that not everyone in the world needs to **know of** you. The ones who do need to **know of** you are those in the community you serve. They need to **know** your desire to serve others, your intent, your commitment, and your integrity. They need to **know** how you operate and if you are a person of your word.

Does your community truly **know** you? They should!

> "The community you serve (i.e., your universe) does not need to be the world. Actually, the more targeted you can make it, the easier it is for you to find your customers and more importantly, for them to find you."

To truly **know** someone, it's important to understand their underlying desire to serve others, as well as their intention, their commitment, and their integrity.

The next two sections focus on the clarity of the audience you serve and how you serve them. It's key to articulate and continually reinforce your desire to be of service, as well as your intent, commitment, and integrity. You'll be guided on how you can make it easy for others to **know** you.

Questions to ask yourself:

1. Do you feel that your community really knows you?
2. Do you have clarity of purpose?
3. Do you have a passion to serve?

THE THREE PILLARS OF CREDIBILITY

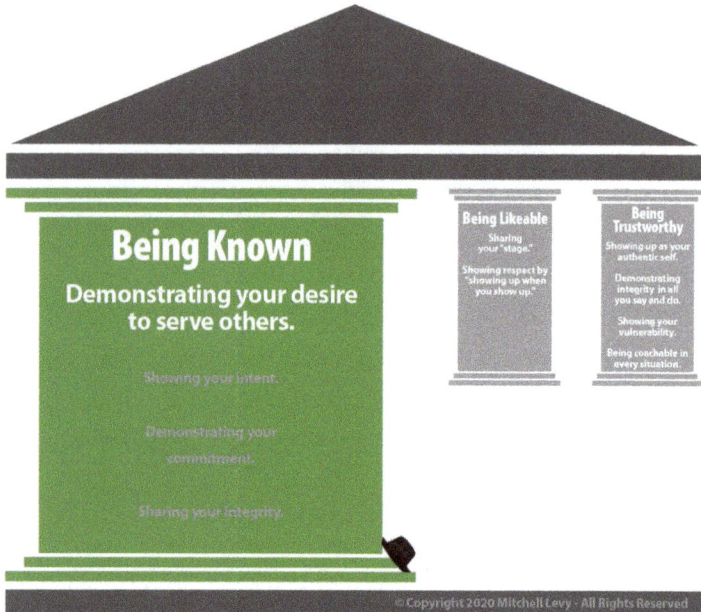

Being Known

Demonstrating your desire to serve others.

Showing your intent.

Demonstrating your commitment.

Sharing your integrity.

Being Likeable

Sharing your "stage."

Showing respect by "showing up when you show up."

Being Trustworthy

Showing up as your authentic self.

Demonstrating integrity in all you say and do.

Showing your vulnerability.

Being coachable in every situation.

Share the AHA messages from this book socially by going to
https://aha.pub/CredibilityNationAHAs.

Scan the QR code or use this link to watch the section videos and more on this section topic:
https://aha.pub/CredibilityNationSVs

Section II

Clearly Articulate Your Audience and Their Pain Point

The credibility research shows that clearly articulating whom you serve and what their pain point is allows you to be more successful. That clarity makes it easy for people to find you, **know** you, and recommend you. It also acts as a compass to guide you in making decisions on projects to take on, partners to work with, and how to present yourself in the physical and online worlds.

That is why the first question in all of the interviews is, "What is your CPoP? What is your customer point of pain?"

Your CPoP—also see **https://MitchellLevy.com/CPoP**—is the specific problem, issue, or concern that your customers (those you serve) have that you can help to resolve.

It's short, memorable, shareable, and begs the response, "Tell me more."

The formula:

1) A CPoP can, but doesn't need to, include the class of clients served.
2) In one to ten words (one to five seconds), what is the primary problem, issue, concern, or aspiration that you address for your clients?

Check out two great compilations of CPoPs:

https://aha.pub/cpops-001

https://aha.pub/cpops-002

Although the formula for creating your CPoP is simple, many of those who were interviewed (98 percent) had a hard time articulating their CPoP with clarity without a little bit of coaching.

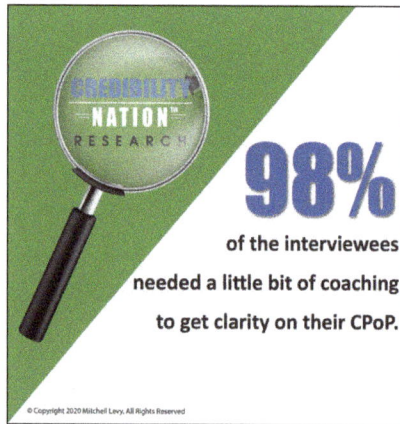

There are two reasons why it's not easy to articulate your CPoP:

1) Brevity and clarity of speech have not been fundamental concepts of the education that resulted from the industrial age.
2) It's been drilled into our heads that our "value proposition" is the first thing we say when we meet another businessperson. The value proposition starts with "I" or "we."

Whether you're talking to a prospect for the first time or reminding someone of who you are and what you do, the first words that come out of your mouth should not be your value proposition. Based on the credibility research, it should be third.

Thank you, Kim Walsh Phillips (**https://aha.pub/KimWalshPhillipsCred**), for sharing number two.

Here's the desired sequence that builds the most trust:

1) CPoP (Customer Point of Pain).
2) WDTW (What Do They Want).
3) Value Proposition.

The first thing you should say in talking with someone is your CPoP. When you have clarity of the audience you serve and the pain point they have, everything falls into place. Who you are becomes clear because it's easier to see whom you serve and how. Your intent and passion to serve come through, as the CPoP allows you to share what you do in the perspective of those you serve.

A good CPoP is memorable, shareable, and begs the response, "Tell me more."

The second thing you should say is in direct response to "tell me more." The ideal response at that stage is WDTW (What Do They Want). The WDTW is typically your product name in the perspective of what your audience is looking to achieve.

The formula:

1. The estimated time to implement the solution.
2. In five words or less, what does your audience want to achieve?

Examples:

- 5-Hour Energy Drink.
- 1-Hour LinkedIn Lead Magnet.
- 5-Minute Close Ratio Booster.

A good WDTW allows you to clearly articulate what you can help your audience achieve.

The third thing you should say is your value proposition. Your value proposition is simply the details of how you help your customers achieve their goals. When you share your value proposition third, you're painting a clear picture of the value you bring to the table.

The formula:

1. Starts with "I" or "we" or the name of the company.
2. Verb (e.g., help, give).
3. Who your market is.
4. What you do to help.
5. How you do that.

Examples:

- I help entrepreneurs increase their sales by creating a sales funnel that is scalable and sustainable.
- We provide marketers with the marketing materials they need to attract more customers.
- THiNKaha helps humans obtain more credibility through books, credreels™, courses, and a membership community.

Going by that sequence (i.e., CPoP -> WDTW -> Value Proposition) can help you make the most of the conversations you're having, as it builds the most trust. Not only that, it also provides you with more clarity when talking about who you are and what you do.

The CPoP not only allows you to effectively start conversations, it also helps you figure out your next steps.

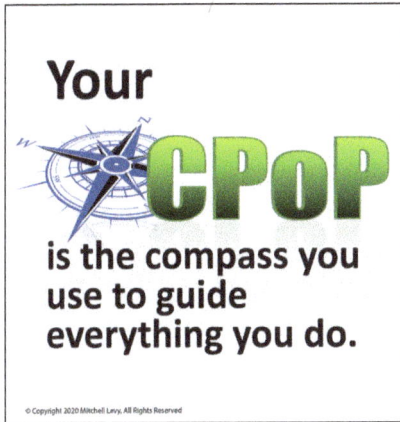

Your **CPoP** is the compass you use to guide everything you do.

© Copyright 2020 Mitchell Levy, All Rights Reserved

When you don't know what your next step is or when you feel like you're deviating from the right path, you just need to go back to your CPoP. Your CPoP will guide you because it is the essence of who you are and what your purpose is.

> "I believe that the CPoP is the key to a happier, more fulfilling life. It guides you on how to effectively communicate who you are while keeping you on the credibility path with what you do and the decisions you make. That allows you to **be known** for who you are and what you stand for and for others to **know** you and to recommend you."

13

Clearly articulating whom you serve and what their pain point is allows you to be more successful. That clarity makes it easy for people to find you, know you, and recommend you. #CPoP #CredibilityNation https://aha.pub/MitchellLevy

---

14

Knowing of you is not knowing you!
How do people get to KNOW you? #CredibilityNation
https://aha.pub/MitchellLevy

15

Your #CPoP acts as a compass to guide you in making decisions on projects to take, partners to work with, and how to present yourself in the physical and online worlds. #CredibilityNation https://aha.pub/MitchellLevy

_____

_____

_____

16

To clearly articulate who you are, you must articulate whom you serve and what their pain point is. Doing so allows you to demonstrate your clarity of purpose. #CPoP #CredibilityNation https://aha.pub/MitchellLevy

_____

_____

_____

17

The #CPoP is the specific problem, issue, concern, or aspiration that your community has that you help resolve. It allows you to articulate who you are by whom you serve. #CredibilityNation https://MitchellLevy.com/CPoP/ -Mitchell Levy

---

18

The community you serve does not need to be the world. The more targeted you can make it, the easier it is for you to find your customers and more importantly, for them to find you. #CPoP #CredibilityNation https://aha.pub/MitchellLevy

---

19

The #CredibilityNation research shows that many successful people do one thing well that is targeted to a specific audience. #CPoP https://aha.pub/MitchellLevy

---

20

If you want more success in business, hone in on your audience and the pain point you address for them, specifically those who you feel need to know about you. #CPoP #CredibilityNation https://aha.pub/MitchellLevy

---

21

Do you know who your customers are? Most people don't. They are those you serve. If you want to be recommended, whom do you want to be recommended to? #CPoP #CredibilityNation
https://aha.pub/MitchellLevy

22

The #CPoP can act as a magnet. It allows you to attract the right people and repel those who are not part of the audience you serve. #CredibilityNation
https://MitchellLevy.com/CPoP/ -Mitchell Levy

23

You don't create a #CPoP to sell the pain. You create a CPoP to give the person listening to you a reason to give you more time. #CredibilityNation
https://MitchellLevy.com/CPoP/ -Mitchell Levy

_____

_____

_____

24

Based on the #CredibilityNation research, 98% of people can't answer this question in 3-5 seconds: "What is your #CPoP? What is your customer point of pain?" Are you in the 2%?
https://MitchellLevy.com/CPoP/ -MitchellLevy

_____

_____

_____

25

1 of 2 Reasons That It's Hard to Articulate Your #CPoP: Brevity and clarity of speech have not been the fundamental concepts of education that emanated from the industrial age. #CredibilityNation https://MitchellLevy.com/CPoP/ -Mitchell Levy

_____

_____

_____

26

2 of 2 Reasons That It's Hard to Articulate Your #CPoP: It's been drilled into our heads that the first thing we say when we meet another business person is our "value proposition." #CredibilityNation https://MitchellLevy.com/CPoP/ -Mitchell Levy

_____

_____

_____

27

The first words that come out of your mouth
(whether it's your first time talking to someone or not)
should NOT be your value proposition.
It should be your #CPoP. #CredibilityNation
https://aha.pub/CPoPvsValueProp -MitchellLevy

28

When you're asked what you do,
saying your value proposition first makes you sound
egotistical and self-centered. You may lose the trust of
those you're in front of. #CPoP #CredibilityNation
https://aha.pub/MitchellLevy

29

Sharing your #CPoP first allows you to be seen as a person who cares about customers (those you serve) by helping them solve their pain points. That is one of the best first impressions you can make. #CredibilityNation https://MitchellLevy.com/CPoP/ -Mitchell Levy

---

30

When you interact with a potential customer, you need to be able to capture their attention and pique their interest. The #CPoP allows you to do that, as it begs the response, "Tell me more." #CredibilityNation https://MitchellLevy.com/CPoP/ -Mitchell Levy

---

31

When you receive a response of "tell me more" to your #CPoP, the ideal response is WDTW (What Do They Want). The WDTW is typically your product name in the perspective of what your audience is looking to achieve. #CredibilityNation
https://MitchellLevy.com/CPoP/ -Mitchell Levy

32

The order for how you share who you are with others (i.e., #CPoP -> #WDTW -> Value Proposition) can truly change the way they perceive you. If done right, it will allow them to see you as a servant leader. #CredibilityNation
https://MitchellLevy.com/CPoP/ -Mitchell Levy

33

Your #CPoP is the compass you use to guide everything you do. Your CPoP will guide you because it's the essence of who you are and your purpose. #CredibilityNation https://MitchellLevy.com/CPoP/ -Mitchell Levy

_____

_____

_____

34

For people to know you, they need to know your: 1) desire to serve others, 2) intent, 3) commitment, and 4) integrity. Are you clearly articulating those four components of who you are? #CPoP #CredibilityNation https://aha.pub/MitchellLevy

_____

_____

_____

35

The #CPoP enables your intent and passion to come
through, as it becomes very easy for you to share
who you are in a memorable and shareable way.
#CredibilityNation https://MitchellLevy.com/CPoP/
-Mitchell Levy

_____

_____

_____

36

By articulating the audience and specific pain
point you serve, you allow yourself to shine. #CPoP
#CredibilityNation https://aha.pub/MitchellLevy

_____

_____

_____

THE THREE PILLARS OF CREDIBILITY

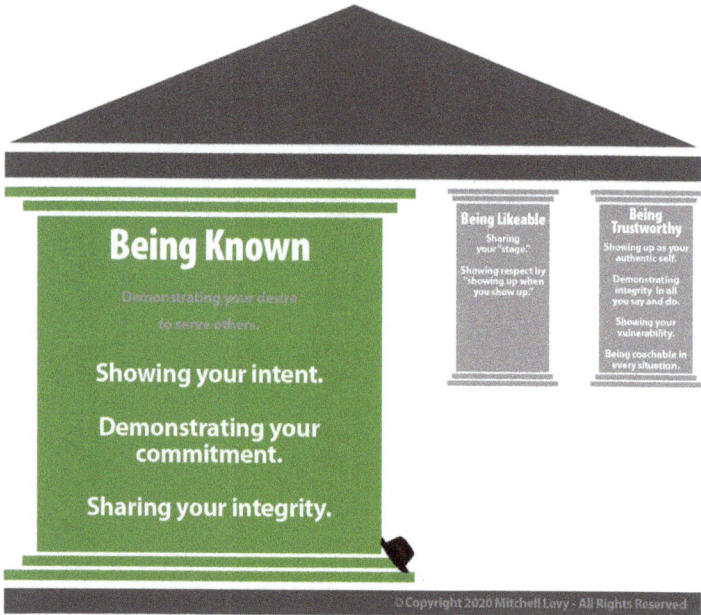

Being Known

Demonstrating your desire to serve others.

Showing your intent.

Demonstrating your commitment.

Sharing your integrity.

Being Likeable

Sharing your "stage."

Showing respect by "showing up when you show up."

Being Trustworthy

Showing up as your authentic self.

Demonstrating integrity in all you say and do.

Showing your vulnerability.

Being coachable in every situation.

Share the AHA messages from this book socially by going to
https://aha.pub/CredibilityNationAHAs.

Scan the QR code or use this link to watch the section videos and more on this section topic:
https://aha.pub/CredibilityNationSVs

Section III

Continually Reinforce Your Presence with Who You Are and Your Credibility

In the previous section, you learned how you can clearly articulate who you are by whom you serve and the pain point you address. Now, it's time to focus on reinforcing the clarity of purpose that you've gained.

What's important for you to understand is that your community can't **know** you from a single interaction. It takes many consistent actions and interactions over time for them to truly understand your desire to serve others, as well as your intent, commitment, and integrity. That's why it's crucial for you to continually reinforce who you are.

There are two areas that you need to reinforce:

1) Your Asynchronous Interactions (not in real-time communication, such as social media, web sites, articles, ads, videos, etc.).
2) Your Synchronous Interactions (same-time communication, in person or online).

Reinforcing both types of interactions allows you to remain consistent in who you say you are. Demonstrating consistency can help your community to **know** and understand you better.

Let's address your **asynchronous interactions** first.

With the rise of technology, almost everyone in the world has the capability to see how you interact asynchronously. It's important to note that it's not just you they can see. They can also see your competition.

How you interact asynchronously (whether it's through your website or social media) should live up to who you are and what you stand for. It should be in alignment with how you want to be seen. This is key in standing high among your competition.

In the 500 credibilty interviews conducted, I got to see the interviewees' asynchronous interactions as part of my preparation. After having our green room conversation and interviewing them, I was shocked to see that 80 percent of the interviewees' asynchronous interactions didn't live up to who they were in real life.

There are three reasons that many people's asynchronous presence suck:

1) How one interacts asynchronously is not perceived as having the same weight as how one interacts synchronously.
2) Most professionals don't have an accountability sponsor for their asynchronous interactions.
3) When a person has an accountability sponsor, they typically don't evaluate how they interact asynchronously in the perspective of credibility while looking for credcrud.

If people do a Google search or go directly to one of your social media profiles, what do they see? If it has a lot of credcrud (written, verbal, and kinesthetic actions taken that subtract from your credibility—also see https://credcrud.com/), your customers will go away and go somewhere else.

For you to be able to truly reflect who you are and what you stand for, how you interact asynchronously needs to be optimized around your CPoP (Section 2).

A powerful asset that came out of the credibility research and can help demonstrate your credibility, is a "credreel™"—also see https://credreel.com/— which is short for "credibility sizzle reel." It is a six to eight-minute interview focused on your credibility. The questions that need to be answered are designed to allow the person watching to **know you** before talking to you.

Now, let's focus on your **synchronous interactions**.

Synchronous interactions are when you demonstrate who you are and your credibility when talking with someone (face to face or virtually). How do you present yourself in an office meeting with prospects and customers? How do you present yourself when you're on a Zoom or Microsoft Teams call?

How you interact synchronously can either solidify or break whatever opportunity or relationship you've already built with others. Showing up when you show up helps you to build good synchronous interactions (see Section V for more detail).

In both your asynchronous and synchronous interactions, you need to understand that a major part of reinforcing your credibility is your team. The CEO, executive team, employees, partners, and customers all support you in reinforcing your credibility.

Many of your customers may make a determination of your credibility based on those in your company they interact with. If your people deliver an UNcredible look and feel and/or experience, that highly reflects on their opinion of you. On the other hand, if your people deliver a "credible" look and feel and/or experience, that also reflects on you.

This is another area where magic occurs.

If all of your people deliver credibly, your credibility not only starts to shine, but it also starts to become a magnet that attracts prospects as those who interact with you and your team start sharing your credust (see Section IV). This truly is a case where the sum of the parts adds up to a greater whole.

> The #Credibility of your employees and their success leads to your success. Are you helping your employees be credible and successful?

When you reinforce who you are in every way possible and your community sees that, it will strengthen their belief and their motivation to reach out to you. That will lead you to the next step.

> "I believe that when you reinforce who you are, it's easier for prospects to see who you are and what you stand for. When they do, it becomes a whole lot easier for you to be known as someone worth doing business with."

37

Once you've successful articulated who you are by whom you serve (i.e., your #CPoP), it's important to reinforce that in a way that your community sees and remembers you. #CredibilityNation
https://aha.pub/MitchellLevy

38

A single interaction is not enough for your community to know you. It takes many consistent actions and interactions over time for them to truly understand your desire to serve others, as well as your intent, commitment, and integrity. #CredibilityNation
https://aha.pub/MitchellLevy

39

Some leaders want to focus their audience's attention on their team rather than on themselves. That is okay, but what's better is for both leaders and their teams to showcase their credibility. #CredibilityNation
https://aha.pub/MitchellLevy

40

Reinforcing who you are means having consistency in how you present yourself in every interaction, whether asynchronously or synchronously. #CredibilityNation
https://aha.pub/MitchellLevy

41

You owe it to your partners, your firm, and those who want to interact with you to present yourself the best way possible not just once, but with each and every interaction. #CredibilityNation
https://aha.pub/MitchellLevy

42

Technology is your friend. You need to make sure that your audience and those you interact with have a positive experience from your website and social media. #OnlineCredibility #CredibilityNation
https://aha.pub/MitchellLevy

43

There are people who use different names in different places on the Internet. That makes it hard, if not impossible, to find you. That's #Credcrud. Make it easy for people to find you. #BeConsistent #CredibilityNation https://aha.pub/MitchellLevy

---

44

It's important to avoid easy-to-fix credcrud (https://credcrud.com) on your website. One such area is having the proper formatting and year of your copyright statement. #CredibilityNation -Mitchell Levy

---

45

Don't shout. Putting your name in all caps is shouting. That makes you look less important, not more important. Avoid #Credcrud (https://credcrud.com). #CredibilityNation -Mitchell Levy

_____

_____

_____

46

Does your LinkedIn profile look good and present you well? 99.5 percent of profiles don't. #CredibilityNation https://aha.pub/MitchellLevy

_____

_____

_____

47

If you're going to use LinkedIn, use it well. If you're not going to use it well, it may be better to remove your profile. #OnlineCredibility #CredibilityNation
https://aha.pub/MitchellLevy

_____

_____

_____

48

For many people, there are aspects of your life that are not on your LinkedIn profile. They may be endearing and memorable enough that someone would want to see them on your profile. #AddThem #CredibilityNation
https://aha.pub/MitchellLevy

_____

_____

_____

49

What are the actions you need to take to get into a one-on-one with your prospect? Having a good LinkedIn profile would help. #OnlineCredibility #CredibilityNation https://aha.pub/MitchellLevy

----

50

Your LinkedIn profile is an automatic extension of yourself. How you present yourself in it is no different than how you present yourself in person. #OnlineCredibility #CredibilityNation https://aha.pub/MitchellLevy

----

51

A credible LinkedIn profile can be one of the differences between you being your potential client's top choice and being second. #OnlineCredibility #CredibilityNation https://aha.pub/LinkedInCourse -Mitchell Levy

_____

_____

_____

52

People do business with those they know, like and, trust. A credreel (https://credreel.com/) allows the viewer to better understand who you are and what you stand for before they meet you. -Mitchell Levy

_____

_____

_____

53

There are many tools you can deploy to allow your employees to demonstrate their #Credibility. Books are one of the best tools on the market and are extremely easy to create and distribute these days. #CredibilityNation https://aha.pub/MitchellLevy

---

54

A great way for you to be known is by having others (particularly customers you've served) share your credibility. Do you showcase written, audio, and video testimonials on your sites? #CredibilityNation https://aha.pub/MitchellLevy

---

55

For prospects to see your business as credible, your employees need to demonstrate their #Credibility. #CredibilityNation https://aha.pub/MitchellLevy

_____

_____

_____

56

You can expand your customer base by demonstrating the #Credibility of your org through your employee base. #CredibilityNation https://aha.pub/MitchellLevy

_____

_____

_____

57

Your prospects do business with those they know, like, and trust. When your employees demonstrate their #Credibility, your awareness, likeability, and trust will grow in the marketplace. #CredibilityNation https://aha.pub/MitchellLevy

---

58

The #Credibility of your employees and their success leads to your success. Are you helping your employees to be credible and successful? #CredibilityNation https://aha.pub/GetYourCredreel -Mitchell Levy

59

If you want to innovate, it's not from the top down.
It's from the bottom up. So, get in the trenches
and work with your people. -Evan Dash
https://aha.pub/EvanDashCred via Mitchell Levy
#CredibilityNation

_____

_____

_____

60

When you reinforce your credibility everywhere
possible and your prospects see that, it will strengthen
their belief and their motivation to reach out to you. It
will lead you to the next step. #CredibilityNation
https://aha.pub/MitchellLevy

_____

_____

_____

BEING LIKEABLE as a Pillar of Credibility.

THE THREE PILLARS OF CREDIBILITY

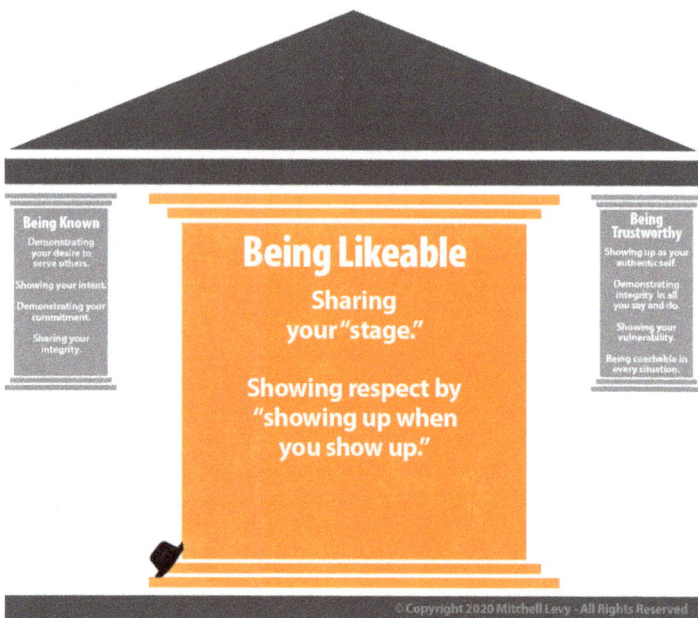

Being Known
Demonstrating your desire to serve others.
Showing your intent.
Demonstrating your commitment.
Sharing your integrity.

Being Likeable
Sharing your "stage."

Showing respect by "showing up when you show up."

Being Trustworthy
Showing up as your authentic self.
Demonstrating integrity in all you say and do.
Showing your vulnerability.
Being coachable in every situation.

© Copyright 2020 Mitchell Levy - All Rights Reserved

Share the AHA messages from this book socially by going to
https://aha.pub/CredibilityNationAHAs.

Scan the QR code or use this link to watch the video on BEING LIKEABLE as a Pillar of Credibility:
https://aha.pub/BeingLikeable

BEING LIKEABLE as a Pillar of Credibility.
Does your community see you as someone who shares the stage and respects others?

Based on the credibility research and external environmental trends, the concept of **being likeable** got flushed out as an important pillar of credibility.

Regarding the external trends, there are three that are significantly changing the nature of work and the competition for that work:

1) The Internet is allowing competition from around the world.
2) Hardware cost has decreased by a significant factor, while SAAS functionality has increased to the point where many tasks/jobs that humans were doing are now being automated.
3) Artificial intelligence is also allowing for the outsourcing of many tasks/jobs that humans were doing.

With all that competition for being **known** and **trustworthy**, what will give you the additional edge to be hired? It's being **likeable**.

Being likeable is a very intriguing pillar of credibility.

It's not 100 percent required, but it offsets **being known and being trustworthy.** I don't need to **like** someone in order to conduct business with them, assuming that I **know** and **trust** them. That said, if there are two choices for whom I should hire and they have an equal weighting of **being known** and **being trustworthy**, the one I **like** will be hired before the one I don't **like**.

The next statement is where **being likeable** becomes most interesting. If I **like** someone, that could compensate for a **being known** or **trustworthy** level that's not exactly what I'm looking for.

Although it's important for your community to **know** and **trust** you, you'll be a lot more successful in business and in life if they **like** you.

The next two sections focus on sharing your "stage" with others while showing respect for those you interact with. Those practices are a great way to go about building and reinforcing **likeability** in your community (i.e., your universe).

Questions to ask yourself:

1. Do you feel that you are generally liked by your community?
2. Do you share credust (see Section IV) at every opportunity?
3. Do you respect those you interact with by showing up when you show up?

P.S. Don't forget to watch the videos at the beginning of each section. They will give you more direct perspective from the author. Also make sure you check out the links to the AHA Messages web page on AHAthat. You will find thousands more there from other amazing people on a very wide range of valuable topics!

THE THREE PILLARS OF CREDIBILITY

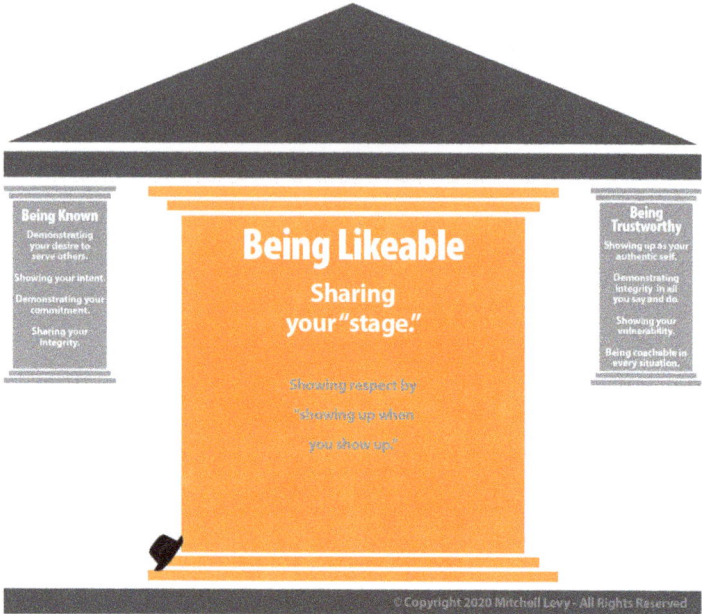

Being Known
Demonstrating your desire to serve others.

Showing your intent.

Demonstrating your commitment.

Sharing your integrity.

Being Likeable

Sharing your "stage."

Showing respect by "showing up when you show up."

Being Trustworthy
Showing up as your authentic self.

Demonstrating integrity in all you say and do.

Showing your vulnerability.

Being coachable in every situation.

Share the AHA messages from this book socially by going to
https://aha.pub/CredibilityNationAHAs.

Scan the QR code or use this link to watch the section videos and more on this section topic:
https://aha.pub/CredibilityNationSVs

Section IV

The Magic of Credust

In the green room conversation after interviewing David Meerman Scott (**https://aha.pub/DavidMeermanScottCred**), he challenged me to come up with a word associated with credibility that doesn't exist and that should be added to the Oxford Dictionary.

I immediately said, "**Credust**." I just wasn't sure if it was with one "d" or two. He said that I should think about whether that was the right word. I did and have also come up with a couple of others as well.

In the conversations I was having with interviewees, there was a common theme of sharing other people's credibility. Credust seemed like the perfect term to represent the act that credible thought leaders were already executing.

> Credust (see **https://credust.com**) is the sparkle that you and the other party receives when you share someone else's credibility.

Imagine having a bag of credust. You reach into the bag to sprinkle credust onto someone else. That's where something magical happens. Instead of the credust in your bag diminishing, it is replenished with more than you started with.

That's the magic of credust.

Although sprinkling credust is easy, it's surprising how many humans don't do it. Reasons include:

1) We've been taught that we need to focus on sharing who we are, and not others, in order to succeed.

2) There's a misconception that when you share other people's credibility, you are giving away opportunities that should be yours.

3) The overall awareness of the law of reciprocity is not commonly understood and deployed by others.

With so many amazing people on the planet, how could you NOT highlight them?

It's great if some of the people you highlight are those you already **know**, **like**, and **trust**. It's even better if some of the people you highlight don't know you yet but get to know, like, and trust you because they recognize that you are sprinkling credust on them.

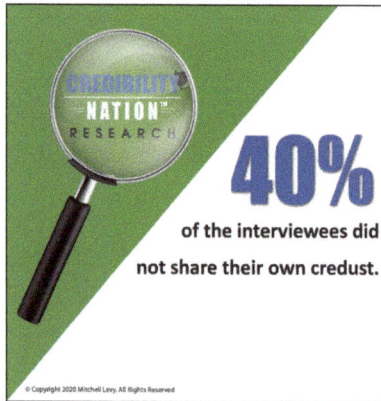

Highlighting someone else's credibility automatically highlights yours. It was shocking that 100 percent of the interviewees didn't share their own credust. There are many reasons for that, and at the end of the day, my fallback answer is that they weren't taught to have the proper mindset. Let's fix that.

An abundance mindset is helpful.

In this case, there's a never-ending resource to share other people's credust.

A function of credust is being a servant leader. It's being able to highlight who you are and what you've learned from others and sharing that with your community.

Spreading credust lifts all boats. The person you're sharing is seen by more people, your community benefits from that knowledge, and your community sees you as a knowledgeable servant leader.

Servant leaders don't sprinkle credust just to be seen by others. They do it because it's the right thing to do. Sprinkling credust is not always visible to your community. It could be that sparkle that happens between two humans who support and show empathy to one another.

Whether it's immediate or in the future, credust leads toward a world that you will want to live in. It's a world where you interact with people who encourage you and allow you to shine. It's a future where it is easy for you to see who plays as a servant leader and who only pretends or doesn't play at all.

Sprinkling credust every chance you get opens up opportunities for establishing good relationships. It allows you to be **likeable** for your servant leadership and your heart.

> "I believe that sprinkling credust on others allows you to shine so brightly that others will naturally be drawn to you and want to build a kinship with you."

61

Highlighting others is not something we were taught to focus on. With so many amazing people in the world and so much info to absorb, showcasing others in your community is a great way to demonstrate your credibility. #Credust #CredibilityNation https://aha.pub/MitchellLevy

---

62

#Credust (https://credust.com/) is what you sprinkle about to grow your credibility. It's when you share the good that your peers are doing in the world, and if appropriate, add your contribution to it. #CredibilityNation -Mitchell Levy

63

Sprinkling #Credust is so easy to do, but not a lot of people do it. That's because we have been taught to stand out and not let others outshine us. That is sad. We should all shine together. #CredibilityNation https://aha.pub/MitchellLevy

64

There are so many amazing people on the planet. If you could highlight those people, showcase them, talk to them, and learn more from them, you would also be highlighting, showcasing, learning, and growing yourself! #Credust https://aha.pub/MitchellLevy

65

When you share other people's credibility, you're doing something valuable for them. You lead, and then there's a good chance that they will #Reciprocate and share your credibility. #CredibilityNation https://aha.pub/MitchellLevy

---

66

There are ways to add to and subtract from your credibility. Are you aware? Check out this #Credust video https://aha.pub/CredustDefinition. #CredibilityNation -Mitchell Levy

---

67

Think about your customer's journey. What partner can you grab who is upstream and downstream of your process to provide value to your customers? https://aha.pub/JayFisetUpDownstream #CredibilityNation @JayFiset via @HappyAbout

---

68

Do unto others as they would want to be treated and share the praise they deserve. #Credust #CredibilityNation https://credust.com -MitchellLevy

---

69

Credible thought leaders not only have something to say, but they also have something to say about what their peers are doing and they add value to the contributions of their peers to the field. #Credust #CredibilityNation https://aha.pub/MitchellLevy

_____

_____

_____

70

There is a never-ending abundance of your ability to share other people's credust. It's not like a bank account with a limited amount of money. You have a never ending supply. So share as much #Credust with integrity as you can. #CredibilityNation https://aha.pub/MitchellLevy

_____

_____

71

If you have a bag of #Credust and you dip into it to sprinkle a little bit of it on someone else, something amazing happens. The bag has more in it than when you started. #CredibilityNation
https://aha.pub/MitchellLevy

72

A function of #Credust is being a servant leader. When you share other people's credibility to your community, you're actually sharing potential solutions to their problems. #CredibilityNation
https://aha.pub/MitchellLevy

73

When you're there to serve others and you're doing it right, you're also serving yourself. #Credust #CredibilityNation https://aha.pub/MitchellLevy

---

74

Spreading #Credust is not always something that's visible to the world. It could be that sparkle that happens between two humans who support and show empathy to one another. #CredibilityNation https://aha.pub/MitchellLevy

---

85

75

Sprinkling #Credust can truly help you and others to live in a world that's full of love and supportive humans. Are you sharing the magic of credust? #CredibilityNation https://aha.pub/MitchellLevy

---

76

Whether it's immediate or in the future, #Credust leads toward a world that you will want to live in. It's a world where you interact with people who are likeable servant leaders. #CredibilityNation https://aha.pub/MitchellLevy

---

THE THREE PILLARS OF CREDIBILITY

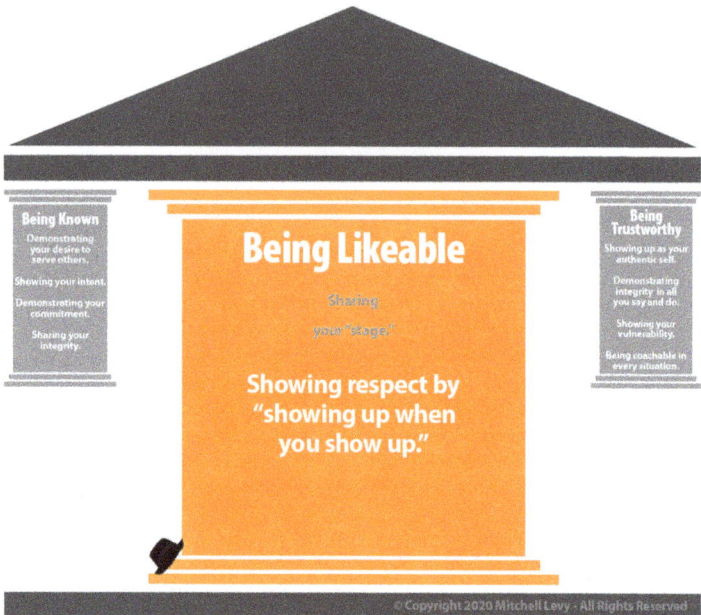

Being Known
Demonstrating your desire to serve others.

Showing your intent.

Demonstrating your commitment.

Sharing your integrity.

Being Likeable

Sharing your "stage."

Showing respect by "showing up when you show up."

Being Trustworthy
Showing up as your authentic self.

Demonstrating integrity in all you say and do.

Showing your vulnerability.

Being coachable in every situation.

Share the AHA messages from this book socially by going to
https://aha.pub/CredibilityNationAHAs.

Scan the QR code or use this link to watch the section videos and more on this section topic:
https://aha.pub/CredibilityNationSVs

Section V

Show Up When You Show Up

In day-to-day business, there are many opportunities to demonstrate your credibility. Do you make the most of them when you have the opportunity?

There are many cases where people show up for an opportunity, but instead of presenting their credibility, they actually present how UNcredible they are.

That is a problem!

If that problem is not fixed, you're not only wasting opportunities, but you're also doing a good job of wasting away as a human.

The solution is to "show up when you show up." That means **coming early**, **being prepared**, and **showing your heart**.

What happens when you're jumping from one meeting to another and you end up being late to all your meetings? You hurt your credibility. You give a negative impression that reflects on your ability to deliver.

The impression you give is that you'll be late and you don't care, that you have no respect for the person you're meeting with. Although you may have been taught to squeeze more into the day, you are actually hurting yourself and achieving less.

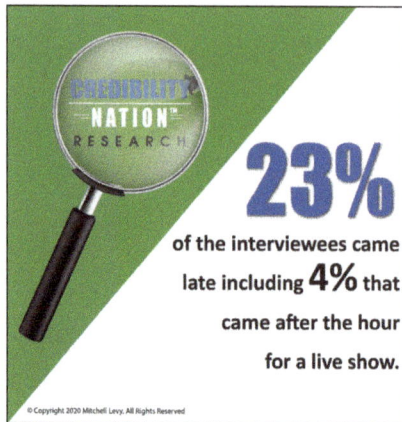

23% of the interviewees came late including **4%** that came after the hour for a live show.

© Copyright 2020 Mitchell Levy. All Rights Reserved

This graphic shows a number that truly is appalling. Not only did 23 percent of interviewees come late (between three minutes and 0 for a live show), 4 percent of those interviewed thought that it was credible to come after the hour to be interviewed on their credibility.

If you show up late for a sales call with me, don't expect to get the sale, and if you continue that behavior, you won't EVER get it.

If you take the time to set up a meeting with another human, show them respect by not just coming on time—**show up early**.

The second important demonstration of credibility is **being prepared**.

> If you've not looked at the LinkedIn profile or whatever platform that's available for whomever you're meeting with before you meet with them, you're stupid.

Being prepared doesn't require a lot of time. At the minimum, you only need to spend five or maybe ten minutes Googling their name and researching whom you're talking to ahead of time. It's simple and easy to do!

If you can come prepared and demonstrate that you've done research on the person you're talking with, you'll understand who they are and how you might be able to serve them.

Initially finding ways to serve should not be about your product or service. It should be about people you may be able to connect them with or third-party content you can share (spreading credust).

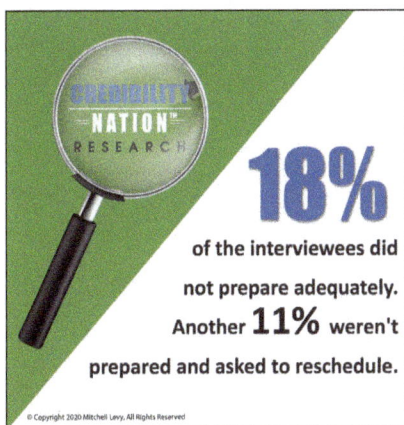

18% of the interviewees did not prepare adequately. Another 11% weren't prepared and asked to reschedule.

© Copyright 2020 Mitchell Levy, All Rights Reserved

Coming prepared is fundamentally important for being likeable and building trust. That shows that you care more about the other person than you care about yourself.

If you get lucky enough to be in front of a prospect, make sure you can communicate quickly, efficiently, and with vigor so that they become energized to talk with you more.

The third important demonstration of credibility is **sharing your heart**. If you don't show up with heart for a person you're interacting with, how can they possibly get to know you? How can they possibly get to **like** you? How could they possibly get to **trust** you?

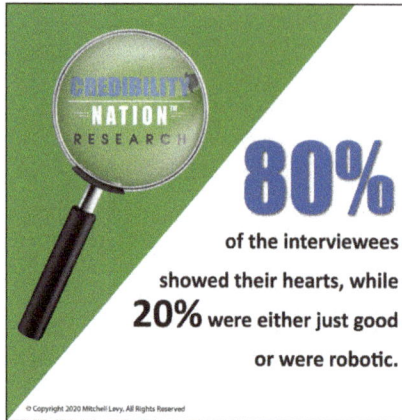

80% of the interviewees showed their hearts, while **20%** were either just good or were robotic.

Showing your heart means that when somebody asks a question, you give them the real answer. You need to be able to demonstrate your true self and not somebody who's acting one way and delivering in a different way.

To make the most of any interaction, you need to demonstrate credibility. You need to show up when you show up. You need to come early, be prepared, and show your heart.

> "I believe that showing up when you show up shows respect to the person you're interacting with. When you show respect and demonstrate your credibility as a human, you allow others to **know**, **like** and **trust** you."

77

There are many cases where people would show up for an opportunity and end up presenting how UNcredible they are. That is a problem! You're not just wasting opportunities, you're doing a good job of wasting away as a human. #CredibilityNation https://aha.pub/MitchellLevy

_____

_____

78

If you #ShowUp for any kind of interaction, SHOW UP! Be prepared and give it all you've got. Make the most of your and the other person's time. #Respect #CredibilityNation https://aha.pub/MitchellLevy

_____

_____

_____

79

What happens when you're jumping from one meeting to another and you end up being late to all your meetings? You hurt your credibility. You give a negative impression that reflects on your ability to deliver. #CredibilityNation https://aha.pub/MitchellLevy

_____

_____

_____

80

To be early is to be on time;
to be on time is to be late; to be late is to be rude.
#MeetingEtiquette #CredibilityNation
-Rich Brenner via https://aha.pub/MitchellLevy

81

Whether you're being interviewed for a show or going
to a meeting, showing up ten minutes early
is showing up on time. #CredibilityNation
https://aha.pub/MitchellLevy

82

Credibility is letting those whom you have meetings with during the day know, as soon as you can, that you need to reschedule due to health or other reasons. #CredibilityNation https://aha.pub/MitchellLevy

---

83

If you're going to show up, show up. If you're going to show up and not be prepared, don't book the meeting in the first place or reschedule. #CredibilityNation
https://aha.pub/MitchellLevy

84

In interviews, both the interviewer and interviewee should be adaptable and flexible for each other. Preparation allows you to do that. #CredibilityNation
https://aha.pub/MitchellLevy

85

On a podcast, it's not just the host's job to know who the guest is. It's also the guest's job to know who is interviewing them. #BePrepared #Credibility https://aha.pub/MitchellLevy

_____

_____

_____

86

Laughing at something funny, even on camera, shows that you're being present in the moment. Don't hold it in. It can increase your credibility and authenticity. #CredibilityNation https://aha.pub/MitchellLevy

---

87

In every interaction, are you letting the person you're interacting with see your heart? We don't recommend those who are not trustworthy or whom you don't feel close to. #ShowUp #CredibilityNation https://aha.pub/MitchellLevy

---

88

If you hire someone to book you for interviews, make sure they help you prepare. Showing up "blind" to an interview is a huge waste of money and effort! Every interaction is important and should be maximized. #BePrepared #CredibilityNation
https://aha.pub/MitchellLevy

89

If you commit yourself to have an interaction with someone you haven't met before, make sure you come with the intention of creating a relationship and not a contract. #CredibilityNation
https://aha.pub/MitchellLevy

90

There are people who don't fit the mold, and it's okay to let them change the rules vs. forcing them into your rules. See https://aha.pub/TeresaDeGrosboisCred for the Teresa de Grosbois interview. #Adaptability #CredibilityNation -Mitchell Levy

---

91

Learn how the person whom you're meeting with wants to communicate and continue to communicate on that platform. (Ex: If you booked a meeting with a calendar tool, use the calendar to reschedule.) #Flexibility #CredibilityNation https://aha.pub/MitchellLevy

---

92

If you show up when you show up, you're there to either 1) teach and share or 2) coach and receive. Either one is fine. #CredibilityNation https://aha.pub/MitchellLevy

_____

_____

_____

93

When you show up at an event, dress the way you want to be seen. That adds to your #Credibility. #CredibilityNation https://aha.pub/MitchellLevy

_____

_____

_____

94

Make everyone you talk with feel like they are the most important. Be "present" in the moment. #CredibilityNation https://aha.pub/MitchellLevy

_____

_____

_____

95

To make the most of any interaction, you need to demonstrate #Credibility. You do that by showing up when you show up (coming early, being prepared, and showing your heart). Are you demonstrating credibility in every interaction? You should! https://aha.pub/MitchellLevy

_____

_____

THE THREE PILLARS OF CREDIBILITY

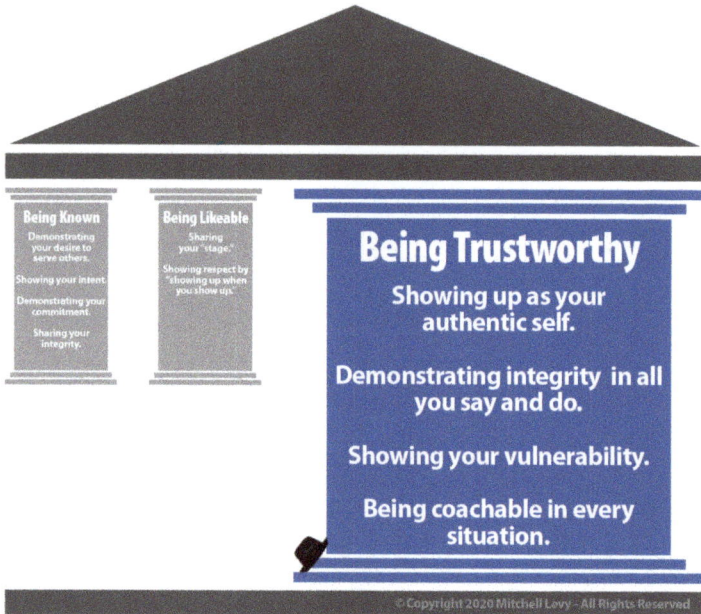

Being Known
Demonstrating your desire to serve others.
Showing your intent.
Demonstrating your commitment.
Sharing your integrity.

Being Likeable
Sharing your "stage."
Showing respect by "showing up when you show up."

Being Trustworthy
Showing up as your authentic self.

Demonstrating integrity in all you say and do.

Showing your vulnerability.

Being coachable in every situation.

Share the AHA messages from this book socially by going to
https://aha.pub/CredibilityNationAHAs.

Scan the QR code or use this link to watch the video on BEING TRUSTWORTHY as a Pillar of Credibility:
https://aha.pub/BeingTrustworthy

BEING TRUSTWORTHY as a Pillar of Credibility.
Does your "community" believe that you can do what you say and that you're continually learning to do it better?

In my TEDx talk, https://aha.pub/TEDtalk, I defined trust as the demonstration of authenticity, integrity, and vulnerability.

Authenticity is being you, the real you, in every situation.
Integrity is being a person of your word.
Vulnerability is being up front about what you know and what you don't know.

Based on the credibility research, I can say that I was only 75 percent accurate in my 2018 TEDx talk. There is one important element that I did not include in that talk, and that is the desire to be coachable and a lifelong learner.

In the industrial age and throughout most of humanity, we learned from those with experience (e.g., the older generation). There was a natural progression throughout the years from novice to seasoned practitioner. That was true when we primarily did one thing our entire lives.

In today's world and moving forward, two key trends are important enough to ensure that the definition of trust is updated:

1. The speed of change is escalating at an unprecedented rate and will continue to increase going forward.
2. Age is not a requirement for knowledge and credibility on a topic e.g., a four-year old often knows a lot more about an iPad than an eighty-year old).

During the credibility interviews, there were humans interviewed who were not able to adjust their mindsets with coaching. Even worse, there was one person who was not interviewed because he flat-out said that he had his way of doing things and was not interested in learning or applying anything I could share with him.

When someone comes across as a know-it-all and is not willing to adjust their style based on the situation, it shows a lack of authenticity, integrity, and vulnerability.

Question number four of the interviews was focused on sharing your credibility. A component of the answer that was flushed out in the interviews was that credible people kept learning (Section VII) and that they shared the credust (Section IV) of those they learned from.

The next two sections focus on demonstrating authenticity, integrity, vulnerability, and coachability. Those practices are a must for **being trustworthy**.

Questions to ask yourself:

1. Do you feel that you demonstrate trust to your community?
2. Do you consistently demonstrate your authenticity, integrity, and vulnerability?
3. Do you allow yourself to be coachable from those you interact with, regardless of their status in life?

P.S. Don't forget to watch the videos at the beginning of each section. They will give you more direct perspective from the author. Also make sure you check out the links to the AHA Messages web page on AHAthat. You will find thousands more there from other amazing people on a very wide range of valuable topics!

THE THREE PILLARS OF CREDIBILITY

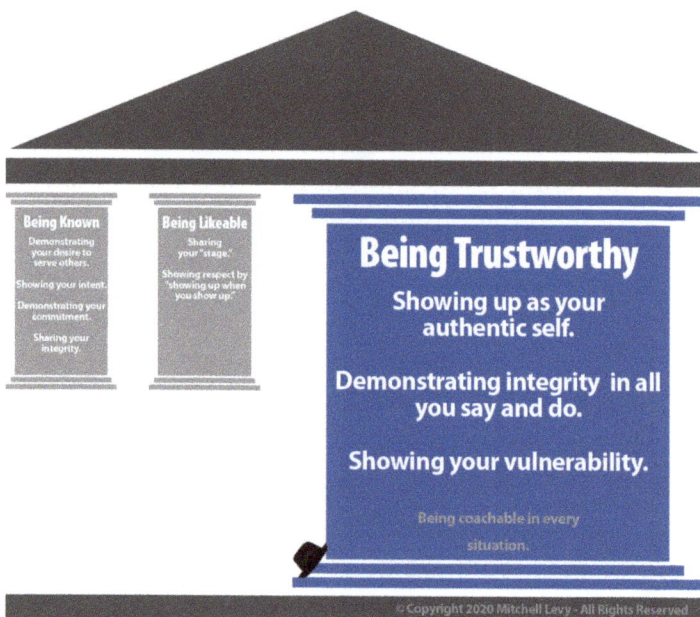

Being Known

Demonstrating your desire to serve others.

Showing your intent.

Demonstrating your commitment.

Sharing your integrity.

Being Likeable

Sharing your "stage."

Showing respect by "showing up when you show up."

Being Trustworthy

Showing up as your authentic self.

Demonstrating integrity in all you say and do.

Showing your vulnerability.

Being coachable in every situation.

Share the AHA messages from this book socially by going to
https://aha.pub/CredibilityNationAHAs.

Scan the QR code or use this link to watch the section videos and more on this section topic:
https://aha.pub/CredibilityNationSVs

Section VI

Reinforcing Your Commitment to Being a Genuine Human

Trust is not gained in one sitting. It is gained through the continual reinforcement and commitment of your authenticity, integrity, vulnerability, and coachability. This section will discuss the first three components of trust, while Section VII will cover coachability and lifelong learning.

Almost all humans know about the first three components of trust; however, many do not make the conscious effort to demonstrate them. Here are three reasons. It's because many humans:

1. Don't have clarity on who they are and how they serve, which makes it hard to demonstrate authenticity.
2. Make promises that they don't mean to execute. They're just saying things to be nice (i.e., the art of execution is becoming forgotten).
3. Are taught that showing vulnerability is a weakness.

Demonstrating authenticity, integrity, and vulnerability takes hard work and practice. Sometimes, it even requires "unlearning" what we learned in the past.

This section discusses how to continually reinforce and commit oneself to demonstrating those three components of trust.

First, let's talk about **showing up as your authentic self**.

Authenticity is one of the potential outcomes of having clarity. One of the things that most humans need clarity about is who their audience is and how they serve them. That goes back to the CPoP (Section II).

The beautiful thing about a CPoP is that it allows you to focus on whom you truly serve. There are people who try to serve a much larger audience than they should or could. At the end of the day, they may become disappointed and frustrated when they find out that they don't serve that wider audience.

If you narrow down the "realistic" audience of whom you serve, you will find that you will be much happier and more effective at who you are and how you serve. A byproduct of narrowing down whom you serve is that it is easier for you and others to see whom you don't serve. Saying whom you don't serve is another potential outcome of clarity and truly demonstrates your authenticity.

Continually reinforcing your credibility doesn't mean that you say your CPoP all the time. It is simply a reflection of how you show up in your community. In your online presence, you need to continually reinforce and make it easy for humans to see whom you serve and how you focus on serving them (i.e., your CPoP).

Next, let's talk about **demonstrating integrity in all you say and do**.

Integrity is simply saying what you do and doing what you say. It's that commitment to deliver on your promises that reinforces your credibility.

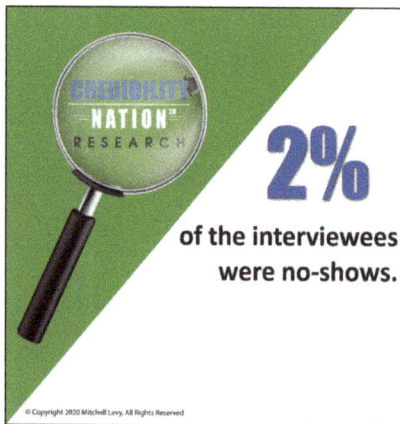

As this is not my value system, I was shocked that 2 percent of the interviewees did not show up.

When you promise to deliver something and you don't do it, no matter what the excuse is, humans lose a little (or a lot of) trust in you. You need to demonstrate integrity in all you say and do. The words coming out of your mouth should not just be the platitude of saying something nice when you don't mean it.

Some people have been taught that if they don't have something good to say, they shouldn't say it unless they're asked. So, when somebody asks for feedback, good or bad, you should say what you really think. It's not that you're being rude. By voicing the hard truth, you're actually helping the person who asked you.

Finally, let's talk about **showing your vulnerability**.

Vulnerability is saying what you know and what you don't know. Showing vulnerability is not a weakness. As humans, we are prone to make mistakes and that's okay. That's how we learn (Section VII).

The first thing you need to do is to admit a mistake to yourself and to others. Those in your community should understand and forgive you as long as you admit your mistakes and show that you're willing to learn and try not to make them again.

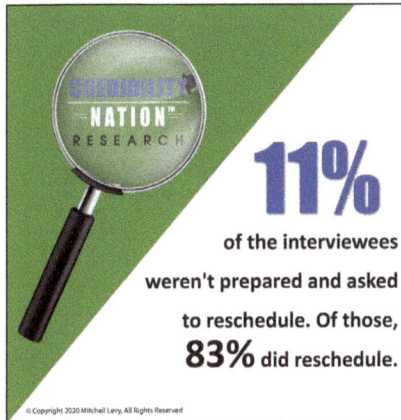

CREDIBILITY NATION RESEARCH

11% of the interviewees weren't prepared and asked to reschedule. Of those, **83%** did reschedule.

It was great when 11% of the interviewees admitted that they were not prepared and wanted to spend more time getting ready and that 83% did make the effort to do that.

When you show vulnerability, you also show that you're authentic and that you have integrity. It shows that you're human and a good, honest human, at that.

Continually reinforcing those components of trust (authenticity, integrity, and vulnerability) shows that you're committed to everything you say that you are committed to. It is a key that unlocks and solidifies relationships with those you interact with.

> "I believe that by demonstrating authenticity, integrity, and vulnerability, you're allowing yourself to be seen as a good and trustworthy human. And that is what will help open doors of opportunities for you."

96

Continually reinforcing and showing your commitment is key to building your credibility. #CredibilityNation https://aha.pub/MitchellLevy

_____

_____

_____

97

One of the best ways to increase your opportunities is by being trustworthy. If your prospects don't trust you, they will not want to do business with you. If they do trust you, they will recommend you to others. #CredibilityNation https://aha.pub/MitchellLevy

_____

_____

_____

98

Trust is the demonstration of authenticity, integrity, vulnerability, and coachability. Do you make it easy for people to trust you? #CredibilityNation
https://aha.pub/MitchellLevy

_____

_____

_____

99

Authenticity is a conscious choice we make to show up and be real in how we live and do business. #CredibilityNation https://aha.pub/MitchellLevy

_____

_____

_____

100

#Authenticity is about being the same person you are whether you are on or off camera. #CredibilityNation https://aha.pub/MitchellLevy

_____

_____

_____

101

Want to lead better? Start with authenticity. It's a great lens to view the world. #AuthenticityInLeadership #CredibilityNation https://aha.pub/MitchellLevy

_____

_____

_____

102

When asked a question that you are not prepared to answer, you can say that you don't know the answer yet and that's okay. #Authenticity #CredibilityNation
https://aha.pub/MitchellLevy

_____

_____

_____

103

When somebody asks you what your #CPoP is, the way you answer should be something that just flows from the heart. Doing so shows authenticity. #CredibilityNation https://aha.pub/MitchellLevy

_____

_____

_____

104

Continually reinforce your #CPoP in your online presence because it makes it easier for people to see who you are and whom you serve. #CredibilityNation https://aha.pub/MitchellLevy

---

105

Integrity is "saying what you do and doing what you say." It's that commitment to deliver your promise. As it's so simple, why don't more people practice it? #CredibilityNation https://aha.pub/MitchellLevy

---

106

Although many people know the "right" thing to do, the art of execution has slipped their minds. #CredibilityNation https://aha.pub/MitchellLevy

_____

_____

_____

107

When you promise to deliver something and you don't, no matter what the excuse is, people lose a little (or a lot of) trust in you. #CredibilityNation https://aha.pub/MitchellLevy

_____

_____

_____

108

The words coming out of your mouth should not just be the platitude of saying something nice when you don't mean it. #Integrity #CredibilityNation https://aha.pub/MitchellLevy

_____

_____

_____

109

#Integrity is doing the right thing, whether or not someone's watching you. #CredibilityNation https://aha.pub/MitchellLevy

_____

_____

_____

110

#Vulnerability is saying what you do know and what you don't know yet. #CredibilityNation
https://aha.pub/MitchellLevy

_____

_____

_____

111

As humans, we are prone to make mistakes and that's okay. There is room to learn from your mistakes and grow. #CredibilityNation https://aha.pub/MitchellLevy

_____

_____

_____

112

Sometimes you need to step out of your comfort zone and be #Vulnerable in order to be #Credible. #CredibilityNation https://aha.pub/MitchellLevy

_____

_____

_____

113

People will understand and forgive you as long as you admit to your mistakes and truly show that you're willing to learn from and not make them again. #CredibilityNation https://aha.pub/MitchellLevy

_____

_____

_____

114

Vulnerability is not a weakness. It is a strength that allows you to connect with other humans beautifully. #CredibilityNation https://aha.pub/MitchellLevy

_____

_____

_____

115

If you're not having fun with what you do, then maybe you don't love what you do. If that's the case, then go find what you do love doing and go do it. #CredibilityNation https://aha.pub/MitchellLevy

_____

_____

_____

116

Have fun every single day. If you love what you do and show that, it gives you credibility. It shows that you're living your purpose. #CredibilityNation
https://aha.pub/MitchellLevy

_____

_____

_____

117

When you love what you do, it's easy to continually reinforce what you're doing and commit yourself to it. #CredibilityNation https://aha.pub/MitchellLevy

118

When you continually reinforce your credibility by demonstrating authenticity, integrity, vulnerability, and coachability, you're making it easy for others to see you as #Trustworthy. #CredibilityNation https://aha.pub/MitchellLevy

THE THREE PILLARS OF CREDIBILITY

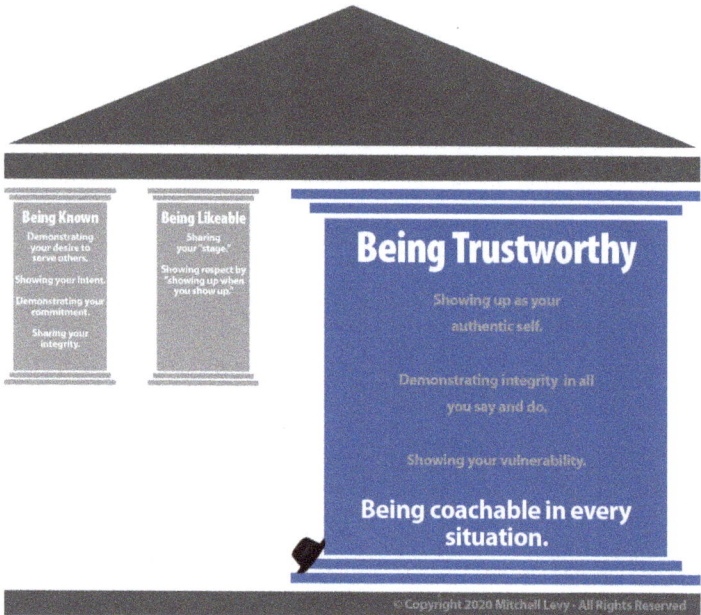

Being Known
Demonstrating your desire to serve others.
Showing your intent.
Demonstrating your commitment.
Sharing your integrity.

Being Likeable
Sharing your "stage."
Showing respect by "showing up when you show up."

Being Trustworthy
Showing up as your authentic self.
Demonstrating integrity in all you say and do.
Showing your vulnerability.
Being coachable in every situation.

Share the AHA messages from this book socially by going to
https://aha.pub/CredibilityNationAHAs.

Scan the QR code or use this link to watch the section videos and more on this section topic:
https://aha.pub/CredibilityNationSVs

Section VII

Continual Growth with Curiosity, Coachability, and Lifelong Learning

As the world continues to change, we need to continually grow and evolve. Continuous growth is crucial for demonstrating credibility in the long run.

I believe that a big part of gaining trust and building credibility is having the desire and motivation to continually grow. When other people see you striving daily to become a better version of yourself, they see your passion, motivation, and commitment to serve others.

If you want to serve others in better ways, you need to become better at what you do. You can accomplish that by:

1. Having unrelenting curiosity.
2. Being open to coaching.
3. Having the desire and motivation for lifelong learning.

First, let's talk about **curiosity**.

Curiosity is a key characteristic for continual growth. By being curious, you will ask a lot of questions and you will be persistent in finding or creating the answers. When you look at how you serve others and you have the curiosity to ask questions—"What do my clients think of my product?" or "What other products or services do my clients need?"—that will lead you to figure out what the answer is and deliver on it.

Now, let's talk about **being coachable in every situation**.

Another important piece of continual growth is coachability. Even though you carry a computer in your pocket or your purse, you don't always have the answers. We are surrounded by people who may have the answers we're looking for.

When you become open to receiving coaching from others, you'll learn a lot more. What's even more beautiful is that the people who coach you will admire you for your willingness to be coached and your passion for being better.

The most shocking encounter I had from the credibility interviews was when one person said that he was not willing to be coached, as he didn't need to learn anything new. My question to you, as a firm hiring credible professionals to support your employees and your clients, why would you hire someone who "knows" it all and is not willing to listen to your employees', customers', or others' opinions?

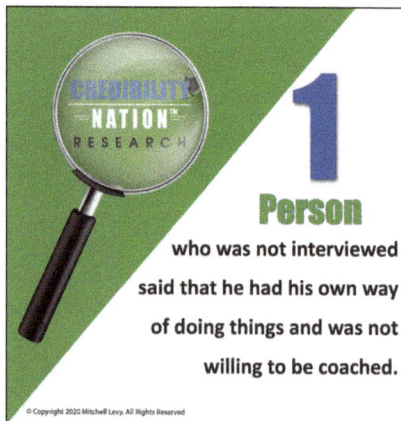

CREDIBILITY NATION RESEARCH

1 Person

who was not interviewed said that he had his own way of doing things and was not willing to be coached.

© Copyright 2020 Mitchell Levy. All Rights Reserved

Finally, let's talk about **lifelong learning**.

Learning is truly not short-lived. It doesn't stop at school. It doesn't stop at home.

Learning is continuous. Every experience we go through has valuable learnings for us. You should be taking those learnings and applying them in your business and your life. If you continuously do that, you'll see that you're a better version of yourself each and every day.

As humans on the path to credibility, providing value is truly our goal. To provide "real" value to those we interact with, we need to continually grow and learn. That will help us deliver what was asked of us and maybe a little bit more.

"I believe that there are valuable lessons and insights we can gain from other humans. We just need to be open to coaching and have an endless passion for learning. In our journey toward lifelong learning, we will earn trust from our actions along the way."

119

The world will continue to change and so should you. You need to continually grow as a human in order to remain relevant and credible. #CredibilityNation https://aha.pub/MitchellLevy

_____

_____

_____

120

Sometimes when things are going well and we're making money, we don't look at the obvious gifts that are given to us. Look around and be open to receiving those pearls of wisdom. #CredibilityNation
https://aha.pub/MitchellLevy

121

There are some experts with skills who think that everyone has them. It's your job to point out how special those skills are. That will help them to understand that the skills they think are normal need to be shared with the world. #CredibilityNation
https://aha.pub/MitchellLevy

122

Sometimes you may know your who, what, and why, but not the how. There are people who can help you with that if you're open to it. #CredibilityNation https://aha.pub/MitchellLevy

---

123

"If I can't do something myself, I'm not credible." Is that always true? Is that ever true? #CredibilityNation https://aha.pub/MitchellLevy

---

124

When you're interacting with someone, do you take their advice because of their grey hair or because they're a fellow human? #CredibilityNation
https://aha.pub/MitchellLevy

_____

_____

_____

125

At every stage of life, there's always an opportunity for coaching from another human. When you are not interested in learning from others, it's time to find something else to do. #CredibilityNation
https://aha.pub/MitchellLevy

_____

_____

_____

126

Are you open to feedback? There are great product ideas that came from customers' suggestions. #CredibilityNation https://aha.pub/MitchellLevy

---

127

Successful people make mistakes and roll with the punches by turning those mistakes into learning experiences or into new ways of conducting business. #Adaptability #CredibilityNation https://aha.pub/MitchellLevy

---

128

When other people see you striving daily to become a better version of yourself, they see your passion, motivation, and commitment to serve others. #SelfImprovement #CredibilityNation https://aha.pub/MitchellLevy

---

129

Sometimes when we show up to share our expertise, we end up learning instead. That's only possible if we're open to gifts that come our way. #CredibilityNation https://aha.pub/MitchellLevy

---

Share the AHA messages from this book socially by going to
https://aha.pub/CredibilityNationAHAs.

Scan the QR code or use this link to watch the section videos and more on this section topic:
https://aha.pub/CredibilityNationSVs

Section VIII

A Life Worth Living

My belief is that there's a possibility to have no separation between work and play (not work). If you love what you do, then you can play all the time, whether you're playing or serving your community. When those in your community see you for who you are and how you are there to serve, it can easily lead to respect, appreciation, like, and love.

Love is a funny word to have in a business book.

Credibility is a set of components that you demonstrate that is not just limited to business. It extends into everything you do. Demonstrating credibility is a way in which you can define your humanity, your existence, and your self-worth.

I encourage you to demonstrate credibility in everything you do. When you do, life will be that much more fun and that much better.

When you come to a meeting (whether business or otherwise) and you demonstrate credibility, it's more likely that a high level of mutual admiration, respect, and love can result even at a first encounter. Follow these three steps to achieve those results:

1. Demonstrate who you are (BEING KNOWN) by demonstrating your desire to serve others, as well as transparently showing your intent, demonstrating your commitment, and sharing your integrity.
2. Demonstrate support of the person you're with (BEING LIKEABLE) by transparently sharing your "stage" and showing respect by "showing up when you show up."
3. Demonstrate how you show up and follow through as a human (BEING TRUSTWORTHY) by transparently showing up as your

authentic self, demonstrating integrity in all you say and do, showing your vulnerability, and being coachable in every situation.

The meetings I have with people when we both "show up" are absolutely spectacular. A bond develops with a mutual respect and admiration that's hard to put into words. It's a feeling that's so powerful that there is just one word that does it justice. It's love.

> It is okay to say to someone whom you've bonded with that you love them. There are silly rules around the world about that, so if you work for a company, check with HR. Whether you can say it or not, it's a feeling that's absolutely worth generating.

That is what I want for you. To love and be loved.

Wouldn't it be amazing to do business with those you love and those who love you back? It would certainly allow you to have a lot more fun and be a lot happier in everything you do.

Credibility can lead to love.

When you have clarity about who you really are and whom you serve and you continually reinforce that by showing up when you show up, you will be going places that you have never imagined possible.

> "When you live your life full of credibility, you will live a life full of love and purpose. And that truly is a life worth living."

130

Credibility is an approach to living life in a beautiful way. It's not something you do for marketing. It's not a game you play just to win. You play to continually improve upon how you serve others. #CredibilityNation
https://aha.pub/MitchellLevy

_____

_____

_____

131

Credibility is not just limited to business. It extends into everything you do. Demonstrating #Credibility is a way in which you can define your humanity, your existence, and your self-worth. #CredibilityNation https://aha.pub/MitchellLevy

_____

_____

_____

132

When you demonstrate #Credibility in everything you do, life will be that much more fun and that much better. #CredibilityNation https://aha.pub/MitchellLevy

_____

_____

_____

133

Having #Credibility doesn't happen accidentally. It happens intentionally. Are you intentional about being credible? #CredibilityNation https://aha.pub/MitchellLevy

_____

_____

_____

134

When those in your community see you for who you are and how you are there to serve, it can easily lead to respect, appreciation, like, and #Love. #CredibilityNation https://aha.pub/MitchellLevy

---

135

What you do should not be different from who you are.
If you need to reinvent yourself as you go through life,
it becomes a whole lot easier if you have built and
continue to demonstrate the attributes associated with
#Credibility. https://aha.pub/MitchellLevy

136

At the end of the day, it's about how you've helped
your clients. How do you show that? #CredibilityNation
https://aha.pub/MitchellLevy

137

Wouldn't it be amazing to do business with those you love and those who love you back? It certainly makes doing business more fun and happier. #CredibilityNation https://aha.pub/MitchellLevy

_____

_____

_____

138

Life provides us interesting opportunities, and it's how we react to those opportunities that defines our character. Is your character #Credible? #CredibilityNation https://aha.pub/MitchellLevy

_____

_____

_____

139

When you demonstrate #Credibility, it's more likely that a high level of mutual admiration, respect, and love can result, even at a first encounter. Is that something you want to achieve?
https://aha.pub/MitchellLevy

140

When you live your life full of #Credibility, you will live a life full of love and purpose. And that truly is a life worth living. #CredibilityNation
https://aha.pub/MitchellLevy

Come join us at Credibility Nation. Go to https://CredibilityNation.com

Appendices

Come join us at Credibility Nation. Go to https://CredibilityNation.com

Appendix A
Bonus AHA Messages from Guests

Appendix A

I had AHA moments with so many of the guests being interviewed. Those that are listed here are just a small portion of the richness of the conversations I had. My apologies for those that are not here.

1. It's like a light switch. It's on and you're in credibility nation. It's off and you're in dubious nation. If you are in dubious nation, that's okay because we're here to help you. On the credibility side, we're here as your ally. #CredibilityNation https://aha.pub/BillWallaceCred

2. There is no #Credibility without walking the talk. If you're not coachable, you can't be a good coach. #CredibilityNation https://aha.pub/SalSilvesterCred

3. A good #CPoP encapsulates your why. If you're walking your why, then you're making it easy for others to see you doing so. #CredibilityNation https://aha.pub/ThomHarrisonCred

4. For leaders, it's important for you to balance the focus on your people with yourself. When you do that, you'll be adding significant value to your org. #CredibilityNation https://aha.pub/DarelynMitschCred

5. Any good quest has an amazing journey associated with it. #CredibilityNation https://aha.pub/RJNicolosiCred

6. In all great things, magnificence is in the details. What I look at are the details in the big picture. Leadership is about clarity. You can't get clarity with simplicity and you can't get clarity without work. https://aha.pub/DwaineCanovaCred

7. Ben Johnson was my mentor and he made $16 billion in his business. He would say, "If you don't show up with your heart, nothing else matters." #CredibilityNation https://aha.pub/DrDougFirebaughCred

8. We need to figure out how to fit into someone else's network and even in their framework and still be ourselves. #CredibilityNation https://aha.pub/NadeneJoyCred

9. Boost your visibility by vividly characterizing a positive action that a person has taken. This will motivate that person to tell others how you said it. #YourQuotabilitySpursSharing #CredibilityNation https://aha.pub/KareAndersonCred

10. Change is a team sport. You can't change without trust. #CredibilityNation https://aha.pub/JoshAllanDykstraCred

Appendix B
Credust Index

Appendix B

Name	Title	Link	Where in the Book Mentioned
Bill Wallace	Founder of Success North Dallas	https://aha.pub/BillWallaceCred	Preface, Page 20
C. Lee Smith	Sales Credibility Expert and CEO of SalesFuel	https://aha.pub/CLeeSmithCred	Acknowledgments, Page 11
Darelyn Mitsch	Founder of Pyramids Coaching Institute	https://aha.pub/DarelynMitschCred	Bonus AHA #5, Page 146
David Meerman Scott	WSJ Bestselling Author	https://aha.pub/DavidMeermanScottCred	Section IV Summary, Page 75
Dr. Doug Firebaugh	CEO of WealthFuel Home Business Training	https://aha.pub/DrDougFirebaughCred	Bonus AHA #8, Page 149
Dwaine Canova	CEO of Zynity and Framework for Leading Institute	https://aha.pub/DwaineCanovaCred	Bonus AHA #7, Page 146
Eran Levy	Director, Head of Thought Leadership & C-Suite Marketing at Cisco	https://aha.pub/EranLevy	Appendix H, Page 167
Evan Dash	President and CEO of Dash Holdings Group, LLC	https://aha.pub/EvanDashCred	Section III AHA #59, Page 69
Fox Beyer	Teacher, Coach, and Author	https://aha.pub/FoxBeyer	Appendix F, Page 161
Jay Fiset	Founder and Creator of JVology	https://aha.pub/JayFiset	Section IV AHA #67, Page 81
Jeffrey Hayzlett	Chairman and CEO of the C-Suite Network	https://aha.pub/JeffreyHayzlett	Appendix F, Page 160
Jonathan Stone	Co-Founder of Impact the Change	https://aha.pub/JonathanStoneCred	Appendix C, Page 152
Josh Allan Dykstra	TEDx speaker and CEO of Helios	https://aha.pub/JoshAllanDykstraCred	Bonus AHA #10, Page 146
Kare Anderson	Author, Quotability Speaker, and Emmy Winner	https://aha.pub/KareAndersonCred	Bonus AHA #9, Page 146
Karin Hurt	CEO of Let's Grow Leaders	https://aha.pub/KarinHurt	Appendix F, Page 161

Name	Title	Link	Where in the Book Mentioned
Karl Hughes	Author, Speaker, Instructor, and Carpenter	https://aha.pub/KarlHughes	Appendix F, Page 161
Kim Walsh Phillips	Founder of Powerful Professional	https://aha.pub/KimWalshPhillipsCred	Section II Summary, Page 39
Nadene Joy	Chair and Founder of The Global Lead 2 Impact Summit	https://aha.pub/NadeneJoyCred	Bonus AHA #8, Page 146
Rich Brenner	One of my mentors	-	Section V, page 93
RJ Nicolosi	Chairman and Founder of Catapult Leadership Lab	https://aha.pub/RJNicolosiCred	Bonus AHA #5, Page 148
Robert Clancy	Host and Producer of the Mindset Reset Show	https://aha.pub/RobertClancy	Appendix H, Page 167
Sal Silvester	Founder and CEO of Coachmetrix	https://aha.pub/SalSilvesterCred	Bonus AHA #2, Page 146 & Appendix F, Page 161
Steve Rodgers	CEO of The Alchemy Advisors	https://aha.pub/SteveRodgers	Appendix F, Page 160
Swami Sadashiva Tirtha	Online Wellness & Stress Management Consultant	https://aha.pub/SwamiSadashivaTirtha	Appendix H, Page 167
Teresa de Grosbois	Chair of Evolutionary Business Council	https://aha.pub/TeresaDeGrosboisCred	Section V AHA #90, Page 99 & Appendix H, Page 167
Thom Harrison	Owner and Coach of Walk Your Why	https://aha.pub/ThomHarrisonCred	Bonus AHA #3, Page 146
Tyler Hayzlett	Chief Marketing Officer of the C-Suite Network	https://aha.pub/TylerHayzlett	Appendix F, Page 160
The THiNKaha Team	-	-	Acknowledgements, Page 11
Those that were interviewed	-	-	Acknowledgements, Page 11

Come join us at Credibility Nation. Go to https://CredibilityNation.com

Appendix C
About the Nonprofit That Credibility Nation
Is Supporting

Appendix C

About the Nonprofit That Credibility Nation Is Supporting:

Jonathan Stone (**https://aha.pub/CredCharity**) is the co-founder of Impact the Change, whose main purpose focuses on ending childhood food insecurity in the USA.

"13.1 million children go to bed hungry every single night, while 50% of food gets thrown away."

Food insecurity has three big downsides:

1. Hunger.

2. Poor nutrition.

3. Emotional trauma.

Food insecurity has only intensified over the years in the USA, due to an ample supply of food that gets removed from the supply chain and goes into landfills.

What Jonathan and Impact the Change does is take shipping containers and turn them into solar-refrigerated food pantries. This enables them to repurpose food in order to provide children with healthier foods (such as fruits, vegetables, and meats) and reduce food waste.

Twenty percent of profit from Credibility Nation is going to charity, and Jonathan's charity is the first one that we're supporting.

Appendix D
The Hierarchy of Sales Credibility
by C. Lee Smith

Appendix D

THE HIERARCHY OF SALES CREDIBILITY

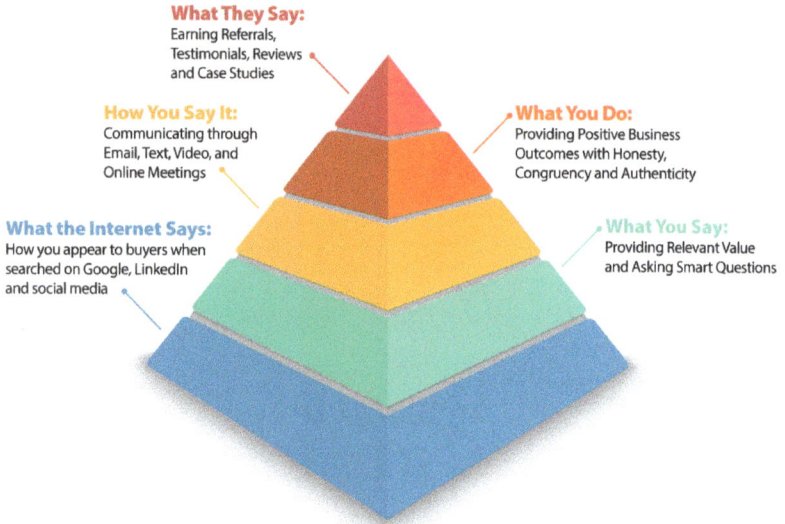

What They Say:
Earning Referrals,
Testimonials, Reviews
and Case Studies

How You Say It:
Communicating through
Email, Text, Video, and
Online Meetings

What You Do:
Providing Positive Business
Outcomes with Honesty,
Congruency and Authenticity

What the Internet Says:
How you appear to buyers when
searched on Google, LinkedIn
and social media

What You Say:
Providing Relevant Value
and Asking Smart Questions

A key component for salespeople to be able to sell effectively is credibility.

Attaining sales credibility is like reaching the top of a pyramid where each tier can help salespeople present themselves to their prospects as someone they know, like, and trust.

Similar to the underlying concepts in Maslow's hierarchy of needs, C. Lee Smith presented *The Hierarchy of Sales Credibility*, in his book *SalesCred*, as a visual representation of what sales managers should keep in mind when training salespeople so they can level up in a step-wise, ascending manner, so to speak, until they reach the pinnacle of what it means to be seen as credible.

This pyramid is not limited to sales; it can be applied to any industry, professional or ordinary people. The path of credibility, leading up to the top of the pyramid, allows them to be seen as credible advisors or individuals in any field.

These tiers are divided into five (5) levels, starting from the bottom of the pyramid as follows:

- **What the Internet Says**
The foundational level in *The Hierarchy of Sales Credibility* is how salespeople appear to buyers when searched online, such as on Google, LinkedIn, and other social media sites. It is crucial that salespeople are aware of their online presence and what the internet says about them. This is essentially the first thing that prospects see or proactively check even before they agree to see them face to face to do business with.

- **What You Say**
How salespeople ask the right questions in order to provide relevant value and solve the problems of their prospects is the next level in *The Hierarchy of Sales Credibility*. This is where salespeople show credibility by giving answers to buyers on what's important to them, what they actually need, and how they overcome objections.

- **How You Say It**
The middle tier in *The Hierarchy of Sales Credibility* is how salespeople are seen as credible by "how they say it" through various communication formats, such as email, text, video, in-person, and online meetings. Prospects and clients often find cues in the way that salespeople speak, write, or talk in order to gauge whether they have authority, professionalism, and confidence in selling.

- **What You Do**
How do salespeople deliver what the buyer wants to achieve? That's the next level in *The Hierarchy of Sales Credibility*. When salespeople reach this tier, it means that they are able to provide positive business outcomes with honesty, congruency, and authenticity, which not many salespeople (or not many people in general) do. Reaching this level means being consistent in delivering what's promised—an admirable trait that strengthens credibility.

• What They Say

This is the topmost level in *The Hierarchy of Sales Credibility*. The path to credibility is ultimately what the customers say as evidenced through referrals, testimonials, reviews, and case studies. C. Lee Smith sums it up beautifully this way, "If you say it, it's bragging. If they say it, it's proof.

In The *Hierarchy of Sales Credibility*, reaching the top level is tantamount to planting a flag in Credibility Nation. Now that the world is faced with a credibility crisis and no longer just a credibility deficit, this visual representation can be useful for sales managers to effectively help their salespeople go up the right path of credibility.

Appendix E
Ten Best CPoPs from Those Interviewed

Appendix E

Ten of the Best CPoPs

- Startup founders who are in panic mode.

- Dreamers who dream bigger than they're achieving.

- Business owners who need their sales to explode.

- Teams demonstrating sub-optimal productivity.

- Family-owned businesses with people issues.

- Women leaders who are juggling.

- Companies with disengaged people.

- Renters who are afraid of being evicted.

- Companies who feel invisible online.

- People who are immobilized by fear.

There were so many amazing CPoPs, it was hard to truly choose the top 10. My apologies for those that are not here.

See more at **https://MitchellLevy.com/CPoP/examples**.

Appendix F
Ten Ways to Enhance Your Credibility

Appendix F

Demonstrate who you are (BEING KNOWN) by demonstrating your desire to serve others, as well as transparently showing your intent, demonstrating your commitment, and sharing your integrity.

Please note that I'm demonstrating the use of credust by choosing AHA Messages from authors that my publishing company has published.

1. Communicating the choices you're making and your intentions with others in the business can inspire them to do the same and support you. #DoTheRightThing -Steve Rodgers (https://aha.pub/IGIPrinciples)
2. Every level you reach in your business will require a new level of commitment. You can't win the game if you don't know why you're passionate about playing the game in the first place. #HeroClub -Jeffrey Hayzlett & Tyler Hayzlett (https://aha.pub/UnlockBusinessPotential)
3. Credibility is not just what you say. It's not just what you do. It's how you act when you have a choice. Do you follow the shiny object, or do you stick with your core values? -Mitchell Levy
4. Spreading credust lifts all boats. The person you're sharing is seen by more people, your community benefits from this knowledge, and your community sees you as a knowledgeable servant leader. -Mitchell Levy (https://credust.com)

Demonstrate support of the person you're with (BEING LIKEABLE) by transparently sharing your "stage" and showing respect by "showing up when you show up."

5. You show up when you show up for every situation (you come early, you come prepared, and you show your heart). -Mitchell Levy
6. Coming prepared is fundamentally important for being likeable and building trust. That shows that you care more about the other person than you care about yourself. -Mitchell Levy

Demonstrate how you show up and follow through as a human (BEING TRUSTWORTHY) by transparently showing up as your authentic self, demonstrating integrity in all you say and do, showing your vulnerability, and being coachable in every situation.

7. Show past your skin. Show what lies within. -Fox Beyer (https://aha.pub/FACTS)
8. Always perform your tasks and do quality work, whether someone is watching or not. -Karl Hughes (https://aha.pub/ACarpentersGuide)
9. Letting people see who you really are and hear what you really mean makes you vulnerable. -Karin Hurt (https://aha.pub/SpeakingtheTruth-AHAbook)
10. There is no credibility without walking the talk. If you're not coachable, you can't be a good coach. - Sal Silvester (https://aha.pub/SCCoaching)

Come join us at Credibility Nation. Go to https://CredibilityNation.com

Appendix G
Ten Things You Do to Hurt Your Credibility
"You Don't Show Up When You Show Up"

Appendix G

You Don't Come Early:

1. You come late to meetings or don't show up at all.
2. You are full of credcrud.
3. Your LinkedIn Profile is not an SEO-optimized landing page for your CPoP.
4. Your website and LinkedIn have pictures, but no compelling videos.

You Are Not Prepared:

5. You don't come prepared for meetings.
6. You share your value proposition vs. your CPoP.

You Do Not Show Your Heart:

7. You ignore the fact that the other person you're talking with is a human.
8. You don't show up every day ready to serve.
9. You position yourself on top of the mountain, not at the bottom.
10. You are not coachable.

Appendix H
Ten Best AHAs from "Being Seen and Being Heard as a Thought Leader"

Appendix H

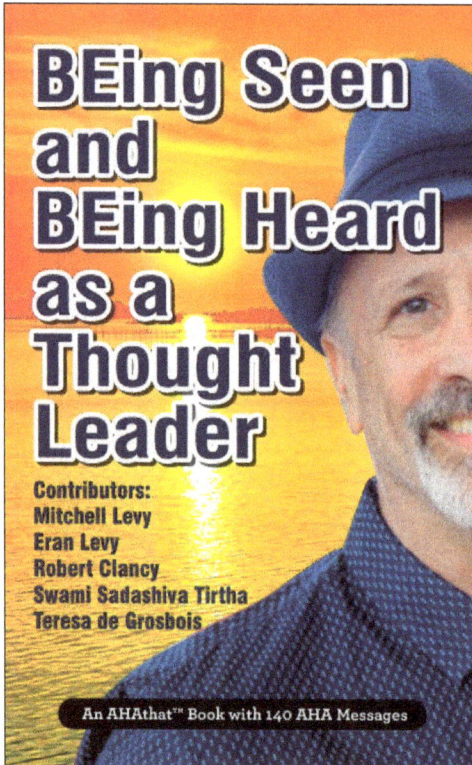

1. Good #ThoughtLeaders are at the top of the mountain; great thought leaders are at the bottom, helping others climb up. @GuideToSoul

2. To position your org as a #ThoughtPartner, bring your key #ThoughtLeaders out front and share their efforts. https://aha.pub/EranLevy

3. Your team has their own ideas. Ask them. Integrate those ideas and march forward together. #ThoughtPartnership https://aha.pub/EranLevy

4. You don't necessarily need to be knocked down to be able to come back up. Be ready. Look and strive for a better life! @HappyAbout

5. To be a leader of leaders, you need to give up the idea that you're the smartest person in the room at any given moment. @TeresaDee

6. You don't have to know how you're going to serve people. You just have to have the intention, commitment & heart to help them. @MonkMedium

7. None of us are ever done; all of us are works in progress. Are you? @TeresaDee

8. Generating trust means that you have to live in a space of integrity, authenticity, and vulnerability. https://aha.pub/TEDtalk @HappyAbout

9. If you love your job, you'll never work a day in your life. If your job is loving, you'll work in happiness every day. @GuideToSoul

10. Be the right voice for the right person at the right time. Don't underestimate what you bring to the world by being you. @GuideToSoul

Come join us at Credibility Nation. Go to <u>https://CredibilityNation.com</u>

Appendix I
Interview Process and Methodology

Appendix I

Mitchell Levy worked with the team to build a process to make it as easy as possible to process the credibility interviews of 500 thought leaders. Here's a visual of the interview process:

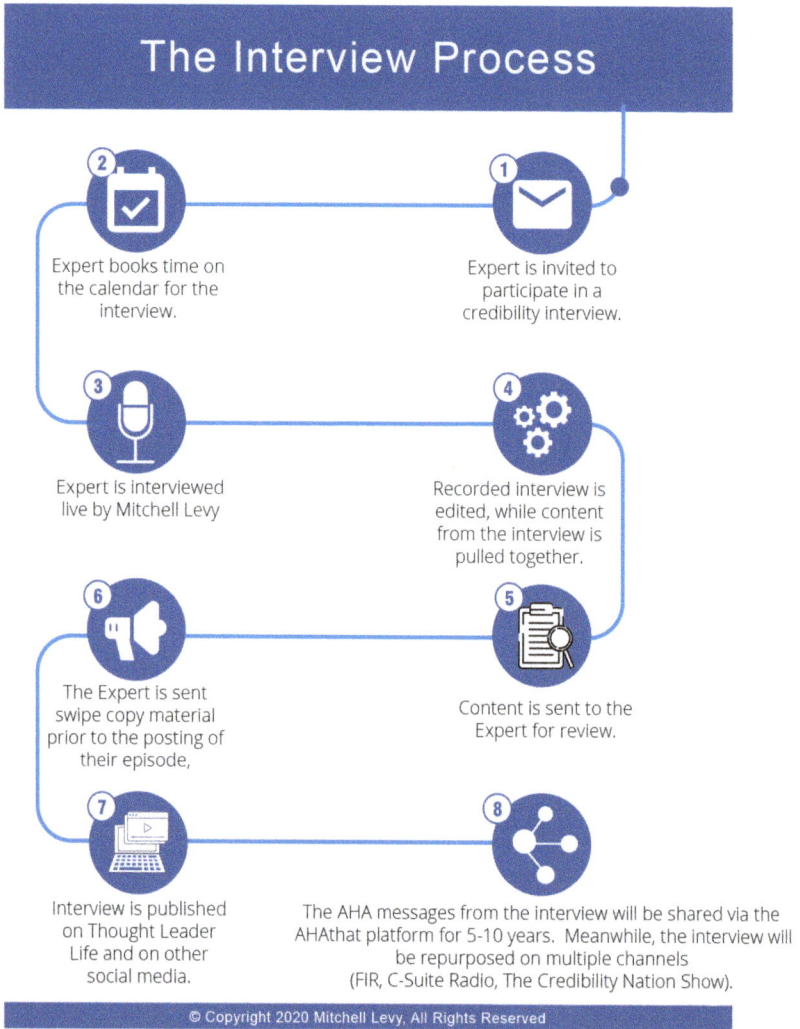

The Interview Process

2 Expert books time on the calendar for the interview.

1 Expert is invited to participate in a credibility interview.

3 Expert is interviewed live by Mitchell Levy

4 Recorded interview is edited, while content from the interview is pulled together.

6 The Expert is sent swipe copy material prior to the posting of their episode,

5 Content is sent to the Expert for review.

7 Interview is published on Thought Leader Life and on other social media.

8 The AHA messages from the interview will be shared via the AHAthat platform for 5-10 years. Meanwhile, the interview will be repurposed on multiple channels (FIR, C-Suite Radio, The Credibility Nation Show).

Now, let's go over each step of the interview process in detail.

Step 1: Expert is invited to participate in a credibility interview.

1.1 Mitchell Levy invited an expert to participate in a credibility interview via LinkedIn.

1.2 Expert checks to see what's involved including the 5 questions asked..

1.2.1 What's your CPoP?

1.2.2 Tell me more!

1.2.3 How do you have credibility to do what you do?

1.2.4 How do you share your credibility?

1.2.5 How do people reach out to you?

Step 2: Expert books time on the calendar for the interview.

2.1 Expert signs up via Calend.ly and filled out a short form that includes their:

2.1.1 50-word bio.

2.1.2 Professional headshot.

2.1.3 LinkedIn profile URL.

2.2 After signing up, the expert receives two emails with info on how to prepare for the interview.

2.3 When the team receives the sign-up form, the following info is transferred into a Google Sheet (which we use for monitoring everyone who signs up):

2.3.1 Date of interview

2.3.2 Name.

2.3.3 Email address.

2.3.4 LinkedIn profile URL.

2.3.5 Professional headshot.

2.4. The team adds the expert as a contact on Nimble (with the same info as above).

2.5 The team adds the expert's bio on a Google doc, along with other interviewees' bios, for Mitchell to use for preparation prior to the interview.

2.6 The team creates a checklist for the week that Mitchell will use during the interview. The checklist consists of:

2.6.1 Interviewee's name.

2.6.2 Did the interviewee come in early (10+ minutes), on-time (4-9), late (3-0), or super late (0-after the hour)?

2.6.3 Was the interviewee prepared?

2.6.4 Did the interviewee present with their heart? Were they just good? Were they robotic?

2.6.5 Mitchell's notes from the green room conversation with the interviewee.

Step 3: Expert is interviewed live by Mitchell Levy.

3.1 The interviewee and Mitchell engage first in a green room conversation while preparing to go live. What often happens is the interviewee gets coaching from Mitchell on how to best present and talk about their credibility.

3.2 Mitchell records the interview via Zoom and streams live on Facebook.

3.3 After the interview, Mitchell sends an email introducing the team that the interviewee will expect to hear from.

3.4 The team then sends the interviewee a link to their Facebook live video to share on social.

Step 4: The recorded interview is edited, while content from the interview is pulled out.

4.1 The video-editing team works on getting the recorded interview cleaned up and adding in an intro and outro.

4.2 Meanwhile, the writing team works on creating an episode summary and 7-10 AHA messages™ (short, digestible quotes) from the interview that will be shared on social.

4.3 Once the episode summary and 7-10 AHA messages™ are completed, they are then sent to copy-edit.

4.4 After copy-editing is done, the content is cleaned up to be sent to the interviewee.

Step 5: Content is sent to the expert for review.

5.1 The clean, copy-edited episode summary and AHA messages™ are shared with the interviewee for review.

5.2 The team also sends the edited video to the interviewee when requested.

5.3 Once the interviewee reviews the content and sends feedback to the team, the team will update the content as needed.

Step 6: The Expert is sent swipe copy material prior to the posting of their episode.

    6.1 Two weeks before the release of the interviewee's episode on Thought Leader Life, the team will send swipe copy material that the interviewee can use to promote the release of their episode.

Step 7: The interview is published on Thought Leader Life and on other social media.

    7.1 Approximately two months after the interview, the episode is published on Thought Leader Life.

    7.2 After appearing on Thought Leader Life, the team strips out the audio and repurposes the interview on multiple channels to be listened to on Stitcher, Spotify, Apple, and Google podcasts: 1) "Thought Leader Life" on the FIR podcast channel, 2) "Mitchell Levy Presents AHA Moments" on the C-Suite Radio podcast channel, and 3) for selected episodes, we feature your episode on "The Credibility Nation Show."

Step 8: The AHA messages are added in an AHAbook on the AHAthat platform to be shared on social for the next 5-10 years.

Overview of the tools we use:

- Audacity
- Calend.ly
- Camtasia
- Dropbox
- Facebook
- Google Calendar
- Google Docs
- Google Drive
- Google Sheets
- LinkedIn
- Nimble
- Vimeo
- Zoom

Come join us at Credibility Nation. Go to https://CredibilityNation.com

Appendix J
Showing Up with Respect for a Live Show

Appendix J

During the interviews, I realized that there was no common understanding of when to show up for a live interview.

For the 500 interviews, the graphics below show how it was measured. The interviewees showed up as follows:

Early: 26%
On-time: 50%
Late: 19%
Rude: 4%

Early	**On-Time**
(10-15 mins early)	*(4-9 mins early)*

Late	**Rude**
(3-0 mins before the hour)	*(1 +mins after the hour)*

Epilogue

Q: What got Mitchell Levy to spend the rest of his life tipping the scale in favor of Credibility Nation over Dubious Nation?

The human who I am now after these 500 interviews is such a different person than I was before.

There's something really powerful about showing up when you show up. I do it now with all of my interactions.

At the end of the day, what came out of the research is an amazingly strong desire to have a human bond, a human connection, and success. To be able to look somebody in the eye, shake their hands, and be able to say, "Hey, this is the business deal and you do this deal whether or not it's contractually obligated." I want to live in that world!

What's wrong today is that we're not taught the right way. Based on the industrial age, we're taught that money and company is more important than relationships with humans, and that's got to change.

How many people are dubious versus how many people are credible? I have to tell you, when you bump into somebody else who's credible, it's such a beautiful experience. Your ability to bond and successfully conduct business is so much easier.

As a result of the credibility research, as a result of everything seen, I have a mission for the rest of my life.

Credibility Nation is losing to Dubious Nation a thousand times over. Before I die, I will tip the scale. That is what this mission is about. It is tipping the scale so that we can live in a world of credibility—where we're living in a world of love and respect and the ability to do the right thing because it's the right thing to do.

I see it as my mission to tip the scale. To allow our kids, our grandkids, and future generations to be able to live a life that is so much more beautiful than today.

To actually live the way we were taught as kids, but never truly lived. To live a life truly worth living.

That's the vision.

Do you see it?

Do you like it?

I invite you to come and join me. Let's tip the scale together.

Scan the QR code or use this link to watch the epilogue video: **https://aha.pub/CredibilityNationEpilogue**

About the Author

Global Credibility Expert Mitchell Levy, is a human whose purpose in life is to serve those who want to be seen as credible and win the war against those in Dubious Nation.

Mitchell has interviewed over 500 thought leaders from across the world on their credibility. This led him to uncover amazing insights on what credibility really is and why it's important in today's world, making him the go-to expert on credibility.

Mitchell has been a Thought Leadership Evangelist for twenty-five years and both a TEDx and Commencement speaker. He also sat as a chairman of the board of a NASDAQ-listed company. Mitchell is an international bestselling author of over sixty books and has created twenty businesses in Silicon Valley, including four publishing companies that have published over 850 books.

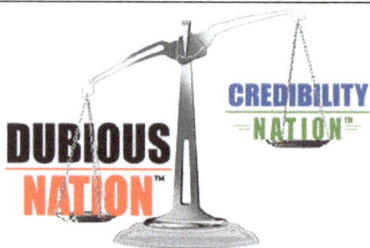

AHAthat®

THiNKaha has created AHAthat for you to share content from this book.

- ➲ Share each AHA message socially: **https://aha.pub/CredibilityNationAHAs**
- ➲ Share additional content: **https://AHAthat.com**
- ➲ Info on authoring: **https://AHAthat.com/Author**

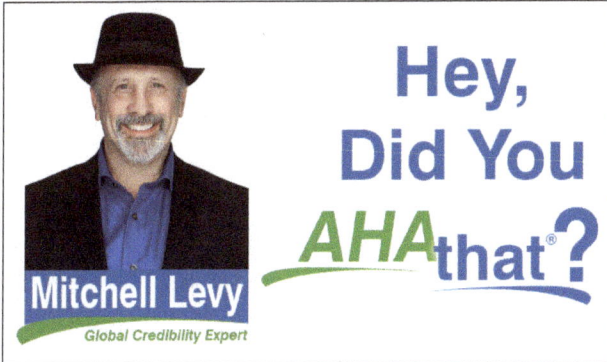

Hey,
Did You
AHAthat®?

Mitchell Levy
Global Credibility Expert